shakespeare's
julius caesar

harold bloom

riverhead books
new york

THE BERKLEY PUBLISHING GROUP
Published by the Penguin Group
Penguin Group (USA) Inc.
375 Hudson Street, New York, New York 10014, USA
Penguin Group (Canada), 10 Alcorn Avenue, Toronto, Ontario M4V 3B2, Canada
(a division of Pearson Penguin Canada Inc.)
Penguin Books Ltd., 80 Strand, London WC2R 0RL, England
Penguin Group Ireland, 25 St. Stephen's Green, Dublin 2, Ireland (a division of Penguin Books Ltd.)
Penguin Group (Australia), 250 Camberwell Road, Camberwell, Victoria 3124, Australia
(a division of Pearson Australia Group Pty. Ltd.)
Penguin Books India Pvt. Ltd., 11 Community Centre, Panchsheel Park, New Delhi—110 017, India
Penguin Group (NZ), cnr Airborne and Rosedale Roads, Albany, Auckland 1310, New Zealand
(a division of Pearson New Zealand Ltd.)
Penguin Books (South Africa) (Pty.) Ltd., 24 Sturdee Avenue, Rosebank, Johannesburg 2196,
South Africa

Penguin Books Ltd., Registered Offices: 80 Strand, London WC2R 0RL, England

SHAKESPEARE'S JULIUS CAESAR

PRINTING HISTORY
First Riverhead trade paperback edition: April 2005
Riverhead trade paperback ISBN: 1-59448-078-8

This book has been catalogued with the Library of Congress.

PRINTED IN THE UNITED STATES OF AMERICA

10   9   8   7   6   5   4   3   2   1

contents

The text of *Julius Caesar,* including the synopsis, is that of the old Cambridge Edition (1893), as edited by William Aldis Wright. I am grateful to Brett Foster for indispensable advice upon the editorial revisions I have made in the text.

—Harold Bloom

harold bloom on
julius caesar

Like so many others in my American generation, I read *Julius Caesar* in grade school, when I was about twelve. It was the first play by Shakespeare that I read, and though soon after I encountered *Macbeth* on my own, and the rest of Shakespeare in the next year or two, a curious aura still lingers for me when I come back to *Julius Caesar*. It was a great favorite for school use in those days, because it is so well made, so apparently direct, and so relatively simple. The more often I reread and teach it, or attend a performance, the subtler and more ambiguous it seems, not in plot but in character.

Shakespeare's stance toward Brutus, Cassius, and Caesar himself is very difficult to interpret, but that is one of the strengths of this admirable play. I say "Caesar himself," and yet his is only a supporting role in what could have been entitled *The Tragedy of Marcus Brutus*. Because Caesar is so crucial a figure in history, Shakespeare is obliged to call the play after him, its highest-ranking personage. The two parts of *Henry IV* are Falstaff's plays, and Hal's, yet they are named for their reigning monarch, which was Shakespeare's general practice as a dramatist. Caesar actually appears only in three scenes, speaks fewer than 150 lines, and is murdered in Act III, Scene i, at the exact center of the play. Nevertheless, he pervades all of it, as Brutus testifies when he beholds the self-slain Cassius:

> O Julius Caesar, thou art mighty yet!
> Thy spirit walks abroad, and turns our swords
> In our own proper entrails.
>
> [V.iii.94–96]

Hazlitt considered Julius Caesar "inferior in interest to *Coriolanus*," and many modern critics agree, but I am not one of them. *Coriolanus,* as Hazlitt first demonstrated, is a profound meditation upon politics and power, but its protagonist fascinates more for his predicament than for his limited consciousness. Brutus is Shakespeare's first intellectual, and the enigmas of his nature are multiform. Hazlitt pioneered in observing that Shakespeare's Julius Caesar does not answer "to the portrait given of him in his *Commentaries,*" an observation that George Bernard Shaw repeated in a severer tone:

> It is impossible for even the most judicially minded critic to look without a revulsion of indignant contempt at this travestying of a great man as a silly braggart, whilst the pitiful gang of mischief-makers who destroyed him are lauded as statesmen and patriots. There is not a single sentence uttered by Shakespeare's Julius Caesar that is, I will not say worthy of him, but even worthy of an average Tammany boss.

Shaw was preparing the way for his own *Caesar and Cleopatra* (1898), which has not survived a century, while *Julius Caesar* has better than survived four. Shakespeare's play has faults, but Shaw's has little else. Shakespeare's source, North's Plutarch, did not show a Caesar in decline; with sure insight, Shakespeare decided that his play required exactly a waning Caesar, a highly plausible mixture of grandeurs and weaknesses.

Though a persuasive representation, this Caesar is difficult to understand. Why is it so easy for the conspirators to murder him? His power pragmatically is all but absolute; where is his security apparatus? Where indeed are his guards? There may even be a suggestion that this Julius Caesar on some level courts martyrdom, as a way both to godhood and to the permanent establishment of the empire. Yet that is left ambiguous, as is the question of Caesar's decline. Shakespeare does not foreground his *Julius Caesar* by reference to Plutarch. He foregrounds it by the affection for their leader not just of Mark Antony and the Roman populace, but of Brutus himself, who has a filial love for Caesar, which is strongly returned. What Brutus communicates to us in one way, Antony does in another, and Cassius in a third, with negative power: Caesar's greatness is not in question, whatever his decline, and however one reacts to his royal ambitions.

Caesar is the grandest figure Shakespeare ever will represent, the person of most permanent historical importance (except perhaps for Octavius, both here and in *Antony and Cleopatra*). Octavius, though, is not yet Augustus Caesar, and Shakespeare evades conferring greatness upon him, in both plays, and indeed makes him rather unsympathetic, the type of the highly successful politician. Though sometimes silly, even fatuous, Shakespeare's Julius Caesar is an immensely sympathetic character, benign yet dangerous. He is, of course, self-centered, and always conscious of being Caesar, perhaps even sensing his deification in advance. And though he can be very blind, his estimate of Cassius shows him to be the best analyst of another human being in all of Shakespeare:

Caesar. Antonius.

Antony.　　　Caesar?

Caesar. Let me have men about me that are fat,
　　Sleek-headed men, and such as sleep a-nights.
　　Yond Cassius has a lean and hungry look;
　　He thinks too much: such men are dangerous.

Antony. Fear him not, Caesar, he's not dangerous.
　　He is a noble Roman, and well given.

Caesar. Would he were fatter! But I fear him not:
　　Yet if my name were liable to fear,
　　I do not know the man I should avoid
　　So soon as that spare Cassius. He reads much,
　　He is a great observer, and he looks
　　Quite through the deeds of men. He loves no plays,
　　As thou dost, Antony; he hears no music.
　　Seldom he smiles, and smiles in such a sort
　　As if he mock'd himself, and scorn'd his spirit
　　That could be mov'd to smile at any thing.
　　Such men as he be never at heart's ease
　　Whiles they behold a greater than themselves,
　　And therefore are they very dangerous.
　　I rather tell thee what is to be fear'd
　　Than what I fear; for always I am Caesar.
　　Come on my right hand, for this ear is deaf,
　　And tell me truly what thou think'st of him.

　　　　　　　　　　　　　　　　　　[I.ii.188–211]

Caesar is accurate, and Antony is not; Shakespeare scarcely could have found a better way to demonstrate the psychological acuity that made Caesar as great a politician as he was a soldier. Yet the same speech indicates one of several gathering infirmities, deafness, and the increasing tendency for Caesar to regard himself in the third person: "for always I am Caesar." Cassius, like many Roman Epicureans, is a Puritan, and embodies the spirit of resentment, unhappy as he is at contemplating a greatness beyond him. Brutus, a Stoic, has no envy of Caesar's splendor yet fears the potential of unlimited power, even if exercised by the responsible and rational Caesar. The soliloquy in which this fear is voiced is the best thing of its kind that Shakespeare yet had written, and is marvelously subtle, particularly where I italicize it:

> *Brutus.* It must be by his death: and for my part,
>   I know no personal cause to spurn at him,
>   But for the general. He would be crown'd:
>   How that might change his nature, there's the question.
>   It is the bright day that brings forth the adder,
>   And that craves wary walking. Crown him?—that;—
>   And then, I grant, we put a sting in him,
>   That at his will he may do danger with.
>   Th' abuse of greatness is when it disjoins
>   Remorse from power; and, to speak truth of Caesar,
>   I have not known when his affections sway'd
>   More than his reason. But 'tis a common proof,
>   That lowliness is young ambition's ladder,
>   Whereto the climber-upward turns his face;
>   But when he once attains the upmost round,
>   He then unto the ladder turns his back,
>   Looks in the clouds, scorning the base degrees
>   By which he did ascend. So Caesar may;
>   Then lest he may, prevent. *And since the quarrel*
>   *Will bear no colour for the thing he is,*
>   *Fashion it thus*: that what he is, augmented,
>   Would run to these and these extremities;

And therefore think him as a serpent's egg,
Which, hatch'd, would, as his kind, grow mischievous,
And kill him in the shell.

[II.i.10–34]

It is one thing to speculate, "So Caesar may," and to follow with "Then lest he may, prevent." But it is peculiarly shocking that Brutus practices the overt self-deception of *"And since the quarrel / Will bear no colour for the thing he is, / Fashion it thus."* That is to acknowledge that there is no plausible complaint to make against Caesar: "Fashion it thus" means to make up your own anxious fiction, and then believe in its plausibility. Caesar, contrary to his entire career, will become an unreasonable and oppressive tyrant, only because Brutus wants to believe this.

Why should Brutus knowingly fashion such a fiction? The instigations of Cassius aside, Brutus appears to need the role of leading the conspiracy to slay Caesar. One could regard Freud's *Totem and Taboo* as a rewriting of *Julius Caesar:* the totem father must be murdered, and his corpse divided and devoured by the horde of his sons. Though Caesar's nephew, Octavius, is his adopted son and heir, there is a tradition that Brutus was Caesar's natural son, and many critics have noted the similarities that Shakespeare portrays between the two. I firmly reject Freud's identification of Hamlet with Oedipus; it is Brutus, and Macbeth after him, who manifest Oedipal ambivalences toward their fatherly rulers.

Brutus's patriotism is itself a kind of flaw, since he overidentifies himself with Rome, just as Caesar does. It is uncanny that Brutus, awaiting the night visit of Cassius and the other conspirators, suddenly becomes a prophecy of Macbeth, in a further soliloquy that seems to belong in the first act of *Macbeth*:

Brutus. Between the acting of a dreadful thing
And the first motion, all the interim is

Like a phantasma, or a hideous dream:
The genius and the mortal instruments
Are then in council; and the state of man,
Like to a little kingdom, suffers then
The nature of an insurrection.

[II.i.63–69]

For a few moments Brutus anticipates Macbeth's proleptic imagination, with "the state of man" echoed by Macbeth in Act I, Scene iii, line 140: "My thought, whose murther yet is but fantastical, / Shakes so my single state of man." Macbeth has nothing like Brutus's rational powers; Brutus has nothing like the Scottish regicide's range of fantasy, yet they almost fuse together here. The difference is that Brutus's "state of man" is more unaided and lonesome than Macbeth's. Macbeth is the agent of supernal forces that transcend Hecate and the witches. Brutus, the Stoic intellectual, is affected not by preternatural forces, but by his ambivalence, which he has managed to evade. His love of Caesar has in it a negative element darker than Cassius's resentment of Caesar. Masking his own ambivalence toward Caesar, Brutus chooses to believe in a fiction, a rather unlikely one in which a crowned Caesar becomes only another Tarquin. But that fiction is not the quality of being that we hear in Caesar's final speech, when he refuses the conspirators' hypocritical pleas that an exile be allowed to return:

Caesar. I could be well mov'd, if I were as you;
    If I could pray to move, prayers would move me;
    But I am constant as the northern star,
    Of whose true-fix'd and resting quality
    There is no fellow in the firmament.
    The skies are painted with unnumber'd sparks,
    They are all fire, and every one doth shine;

But there's but one in all doth hold his place.
So in the world: 'tis furnish'd well with men,
And men are flesh and blood, and apprehensive;
Yet in the number I do know but one
That unassailable holds on his rank,
Unshak'd of motion; and that I am he,
Let me a little show it, even in this,
That I was constant Cimber should be banish'd,
And constant do remain to keep him so.

[III.i.58–73]

Some critics interpret this as absurd or arrogant, but it is true gold; Caesar may idealize himself, and yet he is accurate. He is the northern star of his world, and his rule partly depends upon his consistency. The essence of this speech is its exaltation of a natural hierarchy that has become political. Caesar has no natural superior, and his intrinsic rank has extended itself outward to dictatorship. The skeptic could remark that actually the political here masks itself as the natural, but natural ease is Caesar's great gift, so much envied by Cassius. Julius Caesar, and not Brutus or Cassius, is the free artist of himself in this play, in living and dying. The audience's underlying impression that Caesar is the playwright gives us the unsettling notion of his death as a willing sacrifice to the imperial ideal. I call this unsettling because it diminishes Brutus, whose story then ceases to be a tragedy. Sometimes I entertain the notion that Shakespeare himself—a specialist in kings, older men, and ghosts—played Julius Caesar. Caesar wants the crown, and (according to North's Plutarch) fresh conquests in Parthia; Shakespeare is on the threshold of writing the high tragedies: *Hamlet, Othello, King Lear, Macbeth, Antony and Cleopatra*. The cool disengagement of the dramatist's stance in *Julius Caesar* allows for an inner gathering of the forces, just as perhaps Caesar gathered himself for conquest. Caesarism and tragedy, the first true works in that kind since ancient Athens, will triumph together. The play's authentic victims are Brutus and Cassius, not Caesar, just as its victors are not Mark Antony and Octavius, tuning up for their cosmological contest in *Antony and Cleopatra*. Caesar and Shakespeare are the winners; it is appropriate that this tragedy's most famous lines show Caesar at his finest:

> *Caesar.* Cowards die many times before their deaths;
>   The valiant never taste of death but once.
>   Of all the wonders that I yet have heard,
>   It seems to me most strange that men should fear,
>   Seeing that death, a necessary end,
>   Will come when it will come.
>
>   [II.ii.32–37]

That is not quite Hamlet's "the readiness is all," for Hamlet means something more active, the willingness of the spirit though the flesh be weak. Caesar, gambling on eternity, falls back upon a rhetoric unworthy of him, one that Hamlet would have satirized:

> *Caesar.* The gods do this in shame of cowardice:
>   Caesar should be a beast without a heart
>   If he should stay at home to-day for fear.
>   No, Caesar shall not. Danger knows full well
>   That Caesar is more dangerous than he.
>   We are two lions litter'd in one day,
>   And I the elder and more terrible,
>   And Caesar shall go forth.
>
>   [II.ii.41–48]

That bombast, mocked by Ben Jonson, nevertheless is there to considerable purpose, lest Caesar become so sympathetic that Brutus alienate us wholly. Shakespeare's Brutus is difficult to characterize. To call him a hero-villain clearly is wrong; there is nothing Marlovian about him. Yet he does seem archaic, as archaic as Julius Caesar, in contrast to Mark Antony and Octavius. A stoic tragic hero may be an impossibility. Titus Andronicus, *contra* many critics, was no such being, as we have seen. Brutus may attempt to assert reason against emotion, but pragmatically he stabs Caesar (by some traditions, in the privates), and then endures the mob's initial outcry: "Let him be Caesar," after it has heard his peculiar oration explaining his murder of Julius Caesar, dear friend if not hidden father, but less dear to him than Rome.

Brutus is such a puzzle that he is wonderfully interesting, to Shakespeare as to us. To call Brutus a sketch for Hamlet destroys poor Brutus: he hasn't a trace of wit, insouciance, or charisma, though everyone within the play clearly regards him as the Roman charismatic, after Caesar. Mark Antony has considerably more zest, and Cassius rather more intensity; who and what is Brutus? His own reply would be that Brutus is Rome; Rome, Brutus, which tells us at once too much and much too little. Roman "honor" is incarnated in Brutus; is it not at least as massively present in Julius Caesar? Caesar is a politician; Brutus becomes the leader of a conspiracy, which is politics at an extremity. And yet Brutus has no capacity for change; his curious blindness dominates him until the end:

> —Countrymen,
> My heart doth joy that yet in all my life
> I found no man but he was true to me.

> [V.v.33–35]

These twenty monosyllabic words are very moving, yet they compel the audience to the question: Were you true to Julius Caesar? Evidently Brutus is more troubled than he admits; his dying words are

—Caesar, now be still;
I kill'd not thee with half so good a will.

[V.v.50–51]

Cassius dies, hardly in the same spirit, but with a parallel declaration:

—Caesar, thou art reveng'd,
Even with the sword that kill'd thee.

[V.iii.45–46]

The Ghost of Caesar identifies himself to Brutus, quite wonderfully, as "Thy evil spirit, Brutus," and indeed Caesar and Brutus share one spirit. Shakespeare perhaps did not consider the spirit of Caesarism evil, yet he left that quite ambiguous. "We all stand up against the spirit of Caesar," Brutus stirringly tells his subordinate conspirators in Act II, but do they? Can they? Shakespeare's politics, like his religion, forever will be unknown to us. I suspect that he had no politics, and no religion, only a vision of the human, or the more human. Shakespeare's Julius Caesar is at once human-all-too-human and, as he suspects, more than human, a mortal god. His genius—in history, Plutarch, and Shakespeare—was to merge Rome into himself. Brutus vainly attempts to merge himself into Rome, but he necessarily remains Brutus, since Caesar has usurped Rome forever. I think part of Shakespeare's irony, in the play, is to suggest that no Roman, in good faith, could stand up against the spirit of Caesar, even as no Englishman could stand up against the spirit of Elizabeth. Rome was over-ripe for Caesarism, as England and then Scotland were for Tudor-Stuart absolutism. Harold Goddard charmingly enlisted Falstaff, Rosalind, and Hamlet as Shakespeare's surrogates on Caesar; Falstaff refers to "the hook-nosed fellow of Rome," Rosalind speaks of the "thrasonical brag," the boastful "I came,

I saw, I conquered"; and Hamlet in the graveyard composes an irreverent epitaph:

> Imperious Caesar, dead and turn'd to clay,
> Might stop a hole to keep the wind away.

If Shakespeare identified himself with any of his characters, it might have been with these three, but that takes us no closer to Caesar and to Brutus. Still, I do not trust the scholars on Shakespeare's politics, and no one emerges from *Julius Caesar* looking very admirable. Caesar is coming apart, Brutus is dangerously confused, and there is little to choose between Cassius on the one side and Mark Antony and Octavius on the other: scurvy politicians all. Supposedly Brutus and Cassius stand for the Roman republic, but their actual plans seem to culminate in the butchery of Caesar; their subsequent outcries of "Liberty, freedom, and enfranchisement!" are ludicrous. Brutus, the noblest Roman of them all, is notoriously inept in his funeral oration, particularly when he tells the mob: "As Caesar loved me, I weep for him," rather than "As I loved Caesar." Mark Antony's masterpiece of an oration may be the most famous sequence in Shakespeare, yet it is a half step on the road to Iago. I never quite get out of my ears Antony's finest rhetorical flourish:

> O, what a fall was there, my countrymen!
> Then I, and you, and all of us fell down.
>
> [III.ii.192–93]

There is Caesar's greatest triumph: the promulgation of his myth by Antony's dangerous eloquence. In death, Caesar devours all of Rome.

By the play's end, Brutus, with ambivalent yet "noble" motives, has murdered Caesar. Antony, in vengeance and in quest for power, creates an Iago-like furor: "Mischief, thou art afoot, / Take what course thou wilt!"

Shakespeare, always wary of a state power that had murdered Marlowe and tortured Kyd into another early grave, makes a fine joke of the raging mob's dragging off the wretched Cinna the poet for having the wrong name: "Tear him for his bad verses, tear him for his bad verses," even as Cinna the poet suffers the same fate of Marlowe and of Kyd. Shakespeare, whatever his nonpolitics, did not want to be torn for his good verses, or even for his great ones. *Julius Caesar* was, and is, a deliberately ambiguous play.

2

The Tragedy of Julius Caesar is a beautifully made play, and magnificent in its poetry, and yet it seems cold to many good critics. The greatest of all critics, Samuel Johnson, shrewdly remarked that Shakespeare subdued himself to his subject:

> Of this tragedy many particular passages deserve regard, and the contention and reconcilement of Brutus and Cassius is universally celebrated; but I have never been strongly agitated in perusing it, and think it somewhat cold and unaffecting, comparing with some other of Shakespeare's plays; his adherence to the real story, and to Roman manners, seems to have impeded the natural vigor of his genius.

Johnson was massively right; something inhibited Shakespeare, though I cannot believe that it was North's Plutarch or Roman stoicism. We must look elsewhere, perhaps to the tyrannicide debate, as Robert Miola has suggested. By the time Shakespeare was at work on the play, the popes had excommunicated Elizabeth, and Catholics had plotted to murder her. Shakespeare's

Caesar is at most a benign tyrant, certainly in comparison with the terror afterward practiced as policy by Antony and Octavius. It may be that Shakespeare subtly marks the limits of judgment on tyranny: who is to decide which monarch is or is not a tyrant? The people are a mob, and both sides in the civil war after Caesar's death seem worse than Caesar, which does suggest a pragmatic support for Elizabeth. Yet I am uncertain that the tyrannicide controversy was a prime inhibitor for Shakespeare in this play, wary as he always was of alarming state power.

I suspect that there is a curious gap in *Julius Caesar,* we want and need to know more about the Caesar-Brutus relationship than Shakespeare seems willing to tell us. Caesar accepts death when Brutus, *his* Brutus, inflicts the final wound: "Then fall Caesar!" Plutarch repeats the gossip of Suetonius that Brutus was Caesar's natural son. Shakespeare surprisingly makes no use of this superb dramatic possibility, and surely we need to ask why not. So far is Shakespeare from invoking the father-son relationship (known to all in his audience who, like himself, had read North's Plutarch) that he refuses to allow Caesar and Brutus any significant contact until the murder scene. In their only meeting before that, we get the outrageously banal exchange of Caesar's asking the time, Brutus's saying that it is eight in the morning, and Caesar's thanking Brutus "for your pains and courtesy"! Their very next exchange is their last: Brutus kneels and kisses Caesar's hand ("not in flattery," he fatuously insists) as part of the fraudulent petition to bring Publius Cimber back from exile. Caesar is shocked enough to cry out, "What, Brutus?" and later to note that even Brutus cannot sway him: "Doth not Brutus bootless kneel?" The Caesar-Brutus relationship is thus for Shakespeare a nonstarter; the playwright evades it, as though it would needlessly complicate the tragedy of Caesar, and the tragedy of Brutus.

Unfortunately, this may have been a rare Shakespearean error, for the audience, if it reflects, will sense a missing foreground in the play, as I think Dr. Johnson did. Brutus, in his orchard soliloquy and elsewhere, betrays an ambivalence toward Caesar, which Shakespeare nowhere adumbrates. If the dramatist feared to add patricide to regicide, then he should have given some alternative account of the special relationship between Caesar and Brutus, but he gives absolutely none. Antony, in his funeral oration, says that Brutus was "Caesar's angel" (his darling, perhaps even his genius), and adds that the populace knows this, but gives no hint as to why Brutus was so well beloved by Caesar. Evidently the mob, like the audience, was supposed to know. It is as though Edmund in *King Lear* himself were to gouge out Gloucester's eyes.

Shakespeare perhaps frustrated himself even as he baffles us by this evasion, and I wonder if the absence of the Caesar-Brutus complication does not help account for the baffled quality of the play. As things stand, the mysterious special relationship between Caesar and Brutus makes it seem as though Brutus and not Octavius is the authentic heir to Caesar. Certainly Brutus has a very high self-regard, and a sense of destiny that transcends his own official descent from the Brutus who expelled the Tarquins. If he knows that truly he is not a Brutus but a Caesar, he would possess both a double pride and a double ambivalence. Though Brutus, after the murder, says that "ambition's debt" has been paid, he seems to be thinking of quite another debt. Shakespeare excludes none of this, and includes nothing of it. But the explanation of a father-son relationship would illuminate the ambiguities of Brutus as nothing else does. I turn again to the question: Why did Shakespeare choose not to write this relationship into his play?

At the least, such a relationship would have given Brutus too personal a motive for letting himself be seduced into Cassius's conspiracy, a motive perhaps endless to speculation. Patriotism is Brutus's dominant theme; his function is to save an older and nobler Rome from Caesarism. Shakespeare refuses to foreground why Brutus should be "Caesar's angel," even though, as I will later attempt to show, foregrounding is one of the great Shakespearean originalities, and is the most elliptical element in Shakespeare's art. By refusing to foreground or give any hint as to why Brutus should be "Caesar's angel," the dramatist allows at least an elite in the audience to assume that Brutus is Caesar's natural son. Since Cassius is Brutus's brother-in-law, he can be presumed to know this also, which gives a particular edge to his famous speech that is pivotal in winning over Brutus:

> *Cassius.* Why, man, he doth bestride the narrow world
> Like a Colossus, and we petty men
> Walk under his huge legs, and peep about
> To find ourselves dishonourable graves.
> Men at some time are masters of their fates:
> The fault, dear Brutus, is not in our stars,
> But in ourselves, that we are underlings.
> Brutus and Caesar: what should be in that "Caesar"?
> Why should that name be sounded more than yours?
> Write them together, yours is as fair a name;
> Sound them, it doth become the mouth as well;
> Weigh them, it is as heavy; conjure with 'em,
> "Brutus" will start a spirit as soon as "Caesar".
> Now in the names of all the gods at once,
> Upon what meat doth this our Caesar feed,
> That he is grown so great? Age, thou art sham'd!
> Rome, thou hast lost the breed of noble bloods!
> When went there by an age, since the great flood,
> But it was fam'd with more than with one man?
> When could they say, till now, that talk'd of Rome,
> That her wide walks encompass'd but one man?
> Now is it Rome indeed, and room enough,
> When there is in it but one only man.

O, you and I have heard our fathers say,
There was a Brutus once that would have brook'd
Th' eternal devil to keep his state in Rome
As easily as a king.

[I.ii.133–59]

In a play weighted with magnificent ironies, the most ironical
line may be " 'Brutus' will start a spirit as soon as 'Caesar,' " since
the Ghost of Caesar will identify himself as "Thy evil spirit, Brutus." And there would be a shrewd irony, an audacious one, when
Cassius speaks of "our fathers." Brutus is an unfinished character
because Shakespeare exploits the ambiguity of the Caesar-Brutus
relationship without in any way citing what may be its most crucial strand. *Julius Caesar* has an implicit interest as a study in what
shades upon patricide, but Shakespeare declines to dramatize this
implicit burden in the consciousness of Brutus.

william shakespeare
julius caesar

synopsis

It is the feast of the Lupercalia, and Roman citizens are taking advantage of the holiday to celebrate Caesar's recent victories, but under the seemingly universal rejoicing hidden fires are burning. Two tribunes tear down Caesar's trophies and urge people to return to their homes. Prominent noblemen stand aside and speak of Caesar's arrogance and growing ambition. A soothsayer, gaining the dictator's attention as he passes in triumph, warns him to beware of the Ides of March. Mark Antony, Caesar's henchman, considers the occasion auspicious, however, and three times offers the crown to Caesar who each time refuses it, to the great plaudits of the multitude.

The envious Cassius, the leading intriguer against Caesar, greatly desires to win to the support of his party the high-minded Brutus, whose unassailable character will lend it prestige. He arranges for papers to be thrown within Brutus' reach, designed to show a widespread public alarm over the threat to Roman freedom of Caesar's domination. Brutus is gradually convinced, against his better nature, that Caesar's life must be sacrificed for the common good, but he refuses to consent to the assassination of Mark Antony, whose influence Cassius fears.

The fatal deed is planned for March the fifteenth, but the night before all nature is strangely disturbed and Calpurnia, Caesar's wife, had ill-omened dreams. In the morning the augurers advise and Calpurnia implores Caesar not to leave his house that day. But a tricky conspirator reinterprets the dreams to the dictator's entire satisfaction, and the others, anticipating his hesitancy, call at his house to conduct him to the Capitol. The soothsayer again warns Caesar that the Ides of March are not yet gone, and a friend puts into his hand a scroll revealing the plot which he carries unopened to his death.

In the Senate chamber, Mark Antony is enticed away, and the conspirators crowd around Caesar as though to second a petition which one of them is presenting. Upon Caesar's refusal, first Casca, then the others stab him, and he falls with twenty-three bleeding wounds.

After his own personal safety is assured, the wily Antony affects a willingness to concede the conspirators' point of view, but obtains from the unsuspecting Brutus, against Cassius' advice, permission to follow him in making an address at Caesar's funeral. The crowd, once swayed by Brutus, is now held spellbound by the eloquent Antony who craftily fans their passions to such vows of vengeance and destruction that the conspirators flee the city. Two opposing factions arise. A new triumvirate, composed of Mark Antony, Octavius, and Lepidus, joins forces against Cassius and Brutus, and sets out for the conspirators' camp at Sardis.

Meanwhile Brutus and Cassius quarrel violently over mutual grievances until Brutus informs his fellow general that his wife, the noble and beloved Portia—sister to Cassius—has killed herself in her distraction over the strength of Antony and Octavius. Cassius is so overcome with grief and shock that he yields to Brutus on a vital point of strategy against his own better judgment as a soldier, and their army leaves the safety of the hills around Sardis to meet the advancing enemy on the plains of Philippi. In his tent that night the sleepless Brutus sees the ghost of Caesar who tells him they will meet at Philippi.

When the battle begins, Brutus overthrows Octavius' forces, but Antony forces back those of Cassius. Hard pressed, Cassius sends Titinius, one of his followers, to ascertain whether some far-off troops which he sees are friend or enemy, and, watching eagerly from a hill with his servant, Pindarus, catches sight of Titinius being pulled from his horse. Then they hear a shout of joy. Without waiting for the report, which would have told him of Brutus' success, Cassius orders Pindarus to kill him. When Titinius returns with some of Brutus' victorious soldiers and finds his general dead, he kills himself. The saddened and dispirited forces charge again under the leadership of Brutus, but are driven back by the enemy. His friends having refused his appeal for death, Brutus turns to his faithful servant, asks him to hold his sword and turn his face away. Brutus falls upon it and dies.

historical data

The historical material for the plot of this tragedy is taken from the account of the lives of Julius Caesar, Marcus Brutus, and Marcus Antonius as found in Sir Thomas North's translation of Plutarch's *Lives of the Noble Grecians and Romans,* published in 1579. Shakespeare followed North closely, a large portion of the play consisting merely of the latter's language couched in blank verse. Suggestions for the speeches of Brutus and Antony may have been derived from the English translation (1578) of Appian's *History of the Roman Wars.*

The subject of Julius Caesar was popular among the early Elizabethan dramatists. Among these plays mention is made by Machya in his *Diary* in 1562 of a play *Julyus Sesar,* and by Stephen Gossen in 1582 of a contemporary play entitled *Caesar and*

Pompey. A Latin play on Caesar's death was presented at Oxford that same year.

There is no clear authority for fixing the date of the play, but since it was not included in the list in *Palladis Tamia* in 1598 and is alluded to in John Weever's *Mirror of Martyrs* in 1601, the presumption that it was composed some time between the two dates seems reasonable.

dramatis personæ

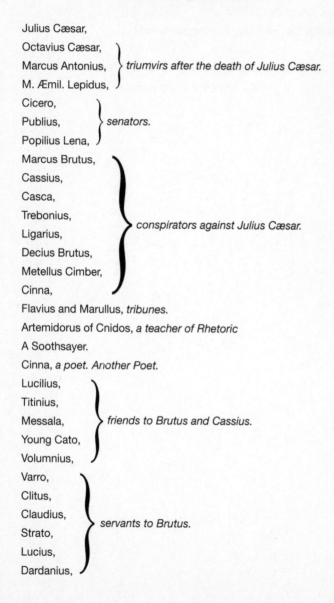

Julius Cæsar,
Octavius Cæsar,
Marcus Antonius, } *triumvirs after the death of Julius Cæsar.*
M. Æmil. Lepidus,

Cicero,
Publius, } *senators.*
Popilius Lena,

Marcus Brutus,
Cassius,
Casca,
Trebonius,
Ligarius, } *conspirators against Julius Cæsar.*
Decius Brutus,
Metellus Cimber,
Cinna,

Flavius and Marullus, *tribunes.*
Artemidorus of Cnidos, *a teacher of Rhetoric*
A Soothsayer.
Cinna, *a poet. Another Poet.*

Lucilius,
Titinius,
Messala, } *friends to Brutus and Cassius.*
Young Cato,
Volumnius,

Varro,
Clitus,
Claudius,
Strato, } *servants to Brutus.*
Lucius,
Dardanius,

Pindarus, *servant to Cassius.*

Calpurnia, *wife to Cæsar.*

Portia, *wife to Brutus.*

Senators, Citizens, Guards, Attendants, &c.

Scene : Rome; the neighborhood of Sardis;
the neighborhood of Philippi.

act 1

scene 1. [*Rome. A street*]

Enter Flavius, Marullus, *and certain* Commoners

Flavius. Hence! home, you idle creatures, get you home:
  Is this a holiday? What, know you not,
  Being mechanical, you ought not walk
  Upon a labouring day without the sign
  Of your profession? Speak, what trade art thou?

First Commoner. Why, sir, a carpenter.

Marullus. Where is thy leather apron and thy rule?
  What dost thou with thy best apparel on?
  You, sir, what trade are you?

Second Commoner. Truly, sir, in respect of a fine workman, I am
  but, as you would say, a cobbler.

Marullus. But what trade art thou? Answer me directly.

Second Commoner. A trade, sir, that I hope I may use with a safe
  conscience, which is indeed, sir, a mender of bad soles.

Marullus. What trade, thou knave? Thou naughty knave, what
trade?

Second Commoner. Nay, I beseech you, sir, be not out with me: yet, if you be out, sir, I can mend you.

Marullus. What mean'st thou by that? Mend me, thou saucy fellow!

Second Commoner. Why, sir, cobble you.

Flavius. Thou art a cobbler, art thou?

Second Commoner. Truly, sir, all that I live by is with the awl: I meddle with no tradesman's matters, nor women's matters, but withal I am indeed, sir, a surgeon to old shoes; when they are in great danger, I recover them. As proper men as ever trod upon neats-leather have gone upon my handiwork.

Flavius. But wherefore art not in thy shop today? Why dost thou lead these men about the streets?

Second Commoner. Truly, sir, to wear out their shoes, to get myself into more work. But indeed, sir, we make holiday to see Cæsar and to rejoice in his triumph.

Marullus. Wherefore rejoice? What conquest brings he home?
What tributaries follow him to Rome
To grace in captive bonds his chariot-wheels?
You blocks, you stones, you worse than senseless things!
O you hard hearts, you cruel men of Rome,
Knew you not Pompey? Many a time and oft
Have you climb'd up to walls and battlements,
To towers and windows, yea, to chimney-tops,
Your infants in your arms, and there have sat
The live-long day with patient expectation
To see great Pompey pass the streets of Rome:
And when you saw his chariot but appear,
Have you not made an universal shout,
That Tiber trembled underneath her banks
To hear the replication of your sounds

Made in her concave shores?
And do you now put on your best attire?
And do you now cull out a holiday?
And do you now strew flowers in his way
That comes in triumph over Pompey's blood?
Be gone!
Run to your houses, fall upon your knees,
Pray to the gods to intermit the plague
That needs must light on this ingratitude.

Flavius. Go, go, good countrymen, and for this fault
Assemble all the poor men of your sort;
Draw them to Tiber banks and weep your tears
Into the channel, till the lowest stream
Do kiss the most exalted shores of all.

> *Exeunt all the* Commoners.

See where their basest metal be not moved.
They vanish tongue-tied in their guiltiness.
Go you down that way towards the Capitol.
This way will I. Disrobe the images,
If you do find them deck'd with ceremonies.

Marullus. May we do so?
You know it is the feast of Lupercal.

Flavius. It is no matter; let no images
Be hung with Cæsar's trophies. I'll about,
And drive away the vulgar from the streets.
So do you too, where you perceive them thick.
These growing feathers pluck'd from Cæsar's wing
Will make him fly an ordinary pitch,
Who else would soar above the view of men
And keep us all in servile fearfulness.

Exeunt.

scene 2. [*A public place*]

Flourish. Enter Cæsar; Antony, *for the course;*
Calpurnia, Portia, Decius, Cicero, Brutus, Cassius, *and* Casca;
a great crowd following, among them a Soothsayer

Cæsar. Calpurnia!

Casca. Peace, ho! Cæsar speaks.

Music ceases.

Cæsar. Calpurnia!

Calpurnia. Here, my lord.

Cæsar. Stand you directly in Antonius' way,
When he doth run his course. Antonius!

Antony. Cæsar, my lord?

Cæsar. Forget not, in your speed, Antonius,
To touch Calpurnia; for our elders say,
The barren touched in this holy chase
Shake off their sterile curse.

Antony. I shall remember:
When Cæsar says 'do this,' it is perform'd.

Cæsar. Set on, and leave no ceremony out.

Flourish.

Soothsayer. Cæsar!

Cæsar. Ha! Who calls?

Casca. Bid every noise be still: peace yet again!

Cæsar. Who is it in the press that calls on me?
I hear a tongue, shriller than all the music,
Cry 'Cæsar.' Speak. Cæsar is turn'd to hear.

Soothsayer. Beware the Ides of March.

Cæsar.   What man is that?

Brutus. A soothsayer bids you beware the Ides of March.

Cæsar. Set him before me; let me see his face.

Cassius. Fellow, come from the throng. Look upon Cæsar.

Cæsar. What say'st thou to me now? Speak once again.

Soothsayer. Beware the Ides of March.

Cæsar. He is a dreamer. Let us leave him: pass.

                    Sennet. Exeunt all but Brutus *and* Cassius.

Cassius. Will you go see the order of the course?

Brutus. Not I.

Cassius. I pray you, do.

Brutus. I am not gamesome: I do lack some part
   Of that quick spirit that is in Antony.
   Let me not hinder, Cassius, your desires;
   I'll leave you.

Cassius. Brutus, I do observe you now of late.
   I have not from your eyes that gentleness
   And show of love as I was wont to have.
   You bear too stubborn and too strange a hand
   Over your friend that loves you.

Brutus.   Cassius,
   Be not deceived: if I have veil'd my look,
   I turn the trouble of my countenance
   Merely upon myself. Vexed I am
   Of late with passions of some difference,
   Conceptions only proper to myself,
   Which give some soil perhaps to my behaviours.
   But let not therefore my good friends be grieved—

Among which number, Cassius, be you one—
Nor construe any further my neglect
Than that poor Brutus with himself at war
Forgets the shows of love to other men.

Cassius. Then, Brutus, I have much mistook your passion,
By means whereof this breast of mine hath buried
Thoughts of great value, worthy cogitations.
Tell me, good Brutus, can you see your face?

Brutus. No, Cassius, for the eye sees not itself
But by reflection, by some other things.

Cassius. 'Tis just:
And it is very much lamented, Brutus,
That you have no such mirrors as will turn
Your hidden worthiness into your eye,
That you might see your shadow. I have heard
Where many of the best respect in Rome,
Except immortal Cæsar, speaking of Brutus,
And groaning underneath this age's yoke,
Have wish'd that noble Brutus had his eyes.

Brutus. Into what dangers would you lead me, Cassius,
That you would have me seek into myself
For that which is not in me?

Cassius. Therefore, good Brutus, be prepared to hear.
And since you know you cannot see yourself
So well as by reflection, I your glass
Will modestly discover to yourself
That of yourself which you yet know not of.
And be not jealous on me, gentle Brutus.
Were I a common laugher, or did use
To stale with ordinary oaths my love
To every new protester; if you know

That I do fawn on men and hug them hard,
And after scandal them; or if you know
That I profess myself in banqueting
To all the rout, then hold me dangerous.

Flourish and shout.

Brutus. What means this shouting? I do fear the people
    Choose Cæsar for their king.

Cassius.   Ay, do you fear it?
    Then must I think you would not have it so.

Brutus. I would not, Cassius, yet I love him well.
    But wherefore do you hold me here so long?
    What is it that you would impart to me?
    If it be aught toward the general good,
    Set honour in one eye and death i' the other,
    And I will look on both indifferently:
    For let the gods so speed me as I love
    The name of honour more than I fear death.

Cassius. I know that virtue to be in you, Brutus,
    As well as I do know your outward favour.
    Well, honour is the subject of my story.
    I cannot tell what you and other men
    Think of this life, but, for my single self,
    I had as lief not be as live to be
    In awe of such a thing as I myself.
    I was born free as Cæsar; so were you.
    We both have fed as well, and we can both
    Endure the winter's cold as well as he.
    For once, upon a raw and gusty day,
    The troubled Tiber chafing with her shores,
    Cæsar said to me, 'Darest thou, Cassius, now
    Leap in with me into this angry flood

And swim to yonder point?'   Upon the word,
Accoutred as I was, I plunged in
And bade him follow; so indeed he did.
The torrent roar'd, and we did buffet it
With lusty sinews, throwing it aside
And stemming it with hearts of controversy;
But ere we could arrive the point proposed,
Cæsar cried, 'Help me, Cassius, or I sink!'
I, as Æneas our great ancestor
Did from the flames of Troy upon his shoulder
The old Anchises bear, so from the waves of Tiber
Did I the tired Cæsar: and this man
Is now become a god, and Cassius is
A wretched creature, and must bend his body
If Cæsar carelessly but nod on him.
He had a fever when he was in Spain,
And when the fit was on him, I did mark
How he did shake. 'Tis true, this god did shake;
His coward lips did from their colour fly,
And that same eye whose bend doth awe the world
Did lose his lustre. I did hear him groan:
Ay, and that tongue of his that bade the Romans
Mark him and write his speeches in their books,
Alas, it cried, 'Give me some drink, Titinius,'
As a sick girl. Ye gods! It doth amaze me
A man of such a feeble temper should
So get the start of the majestic world
And bear the palm alone.

Shout. Flourish.

Brutus. Another general shout!
   I do believe that these applauses are
   For some new honours that are heap'd on Cæsar.

Cassius. Why, man, he doth bestride the narrow world
    Like a Colossus, and we petty men
    Walk under his huge legs and peep about
    To find ourselves dishonourable graves.
    Men at some time are masters of their fates.
    The fault, dear Brutus, is not in our stars,
    But in ourselves, that we are underlings.
    'Brutus' and 'Cæsar': what should be in that 'Cæsar'?
    Why should that name be sounded more than yours?
    Write them together, yours is as fair a name;
    Sound them, it doth become the mouth as well;
    Weigh, them, it is as heavy; conjure with 'em,
    'Brutus' will start a spirit as soon as 'Cæsar'.
    Now, in the names of all the gods at once,
    Upon what meat doth this our Cæsar feed
    That he is grown so great? Age, thou art shamed!
    Rome, thou hast lost the breed of noble bloods!
    When went there by an age, since the great flood,
    But it was famed with more than with one man?
    When could they say till now that talk'd of Rome
    That her wide walls encompass'd but one man?
    Now is it Rome indeed, and room enough,
    When there is in it but one only man.
    O, you and I have heard our fathers say
    There was a Brutus once that would have brook'd
    Th' eternal devil to keep his state in Rome
    As easily as a king.

Brutus. That you do love me, I am nothing jealous;
    What you would work me to, I have some aim:
    How I have thought of this and of these times,
    I shall recount hereafter. For this present,
    I would not, so with love I might entreat you,

Be any further moved. What you have said
I will consider; what you have to say
I will with patience hear, and find a time
Both meet to hear and answer such high things.
Till then, my noble friend, chew upon this:
Brutus had rather be a villager
Than to repute himself a son of Rome
Under these hard conditions as this time
Is like to lay upon us.

Cassius. I am glad that my weak words
Have struck but thus much show of fire from Brutus.

Brutus. The games are done, and Cæsar is returning.

Cassius. As they pass by, pluck Casca by the sleeve,
And he will, after his sour fashion, tell you
What hath proceeded worthy note today.

     Re-enter Cæsar *and his Train*

Brutus. I will do so: but, look you, Cassius,
The angry spot doth glow on Cæsar's brow,
And all the rest look like a chidden train:
Calpurnia's cheek is pale, and Cicero
Looks with such ferret and such fiery eyes
As we have seen him in the Capitol,
Being cross'd in conference by some senators.

Cassius. Casca will tell us what the matter is.

Cæsar. Antonius!

Antony. Cæsar?

Cæsar. Let me have men about me that are fat,
Sleek-headed men, and such as sleep a' nights:
Yond Cassius has a lean and hungry look.
He thinks too much: such men are dangerous.

Antony. Fear him not, Cæsar; he's not dangerous.
  He is a noble Roman, and well given.

Cæsar. Would he were fatter! But I fear him not:
  Yet if my name were liable to fear,
  I do not know the man I should avoid
  So soon as that spare Cassius. He reads much,
  He is a great observer, and he looks
  Quite through the deeds of men. He loves no plays
  As thou dost, Antony; he hears no music.
  Seldom he smiles, and smiles in such a sort
  As if he mock'd himself, and scorn'd his spirit
  That could be moved to smile at any thing.
  Such men as he be never at heart's ease
  Whiles they behold a greater than themselves,
  And therefore are they very dangerous.
  I rather tell thee what is to be fear'd
  Than what I fear, for always I am Cæsar.
  Come on my right hand, for this ear is deaf,
  And tell me truly what thou think'st of him.
                    Sennet. Exeunt Cæsar *and all his Train but* Casca.

Casca. You pull'd me by the cloak. Would you speak with me?

Brutus. Ay, Casca; tell us what hath chanced today
  That Cæsar looks so sad.

Casca. Why, you were with him, were you not?

Brutus. I should not then ask Casca what had chanced.

Casca. Why, there was a crown offered him, and being offered
  him, he put it by with the back of his hand, thus: and then
  the people fell a-shouting.

Brutus. What was the second noise for?

Casca. Why, for that too.

Cassius. They shouted thrice: what was the last cry for?

Casca. Why, for that too.

Brutus. Was the crown offered him thrice?

Casca. Ay, marry, was't, and he put it by thrice, every time gentler than other; and at every putting-by mine honest neighbours shouted.

Cassius. Who offered him the crown?

Casca. Why, Antony.

Brutus. Tell us the manner of it, gentle Casca.

Casca. I can as well be hang'd as tell the manner of it. It was mere foolery; I did not mark it. I saw Mark Antony offer him a crown—yet 'twas not a crown neither, 'twas one of these coronets—and, as I told you, he put it by once: but for all that, to my thinking, he would fain have had it. Then he offered it to him again; then he put it by again: but, to my thinking, he was very loath to lay his fingers off it. And then he offered it the third time; he put it the third time by: and still as he refused it, the rabblement hooted and clapped their chopped hands and threw up their sweaty night-caps and uttered such a deal of stinking breath because Cæsar refused the crown, that it had almost choked Cæsar; for he swooned and fell down at it. And for mine own part, I durst not laugh, for fear of opening my lips and receiving the bad air.

Cassius. But, soft, I pray you: what, did Cæsar swoon?

Casca. He fell down in the market-place and foamed at mouth and was speechless.

Brutus. 'Tis very like: he hath the falling-sickness.

Cassius. No, Cæsar hath it not: but you, and I,
And honest Casca, we have the falling-sickness.

Casca. I know not what you mean by that, but I am sure Cæsar fell down. If the tag-rag people did not clap him and hiss him according as he pleased and displeased them, as they use to do the players in the theatre, I am no true man.

Brutus. What said he when he came unto himself?

Casca. Marry, before he fell down, when he perceived the common herd was glad he refused the crown, he plucked me ope his doublet and offered them his throat to cut. And I had been a man of any occupation, if I would not have taken him at a word, I would I might go to hell among the rogues. And so he fell. When he came to himself again, he said, if he had done or said any thing amiss, he desired their worships to think it was his infirmity. Three or four wenches, where I stood, cried 'Alas, good soul!' and forgave him with all their hearts. But there's no heed to be taken of them; if Cæsar had stabbed their mothers, they would have done no less.

Brutus. And after that, he came thus sad away?

Casca. Ay.

Cassius. Did Cicero say any thing?

Casca. Ay, he spoke Greek.

Cassius. To what effect?

Casca. Nay, an I tell you that, I'll ne'er look you i' the face again. But those that understood him smiled at one another and shook their heads; but for mine own part, it was Greek to me. I could tell you more news too: Marullus and Flavius, for pulling scarfs off Cæsar's images, are put to silence. Fare you well. There was more foolery yet, if I could remember it.

Cassius. Will you sup with me tonight, Casca?

Casca. No, I am promised forth.

Cassius. Will you dine with me tomorrow?

Casca. Ay, if I be alive, and your mind hold, and your dinner
worth the eating.

Cassius. Good. I will expect you.

Casca. Do so. Farewell, both.

Exit.

Brutus. What a blunt fellow is this grown to be!
He was quick mettle when he went to school.

Cassius. So is he now, in execution
Of any bold or noble enterprise,
However he puts on this tardy form.
This rudeness is a sauce to his good wit,
Which gives men stomach to digest his words
With better appetite.

Brutus. And so it is. For this time I will leave you.
Tomorrow, if you please to speak with me,
I will come home to you, or if you will,
Come home to me and I will wait for you.

Cassius. I will do so: till then, think of the world.

Exit Brutus.

Well, Brutus, thou art noble, yet I see
Thy honourable metal may be wrought
From that it is disposed. Therefore it is meet
That noble minds keep ever with their likes;
For who so firm that cannot be seduced?
Cæsar doth bear me hard, but he loves Brutus.
If I were Brutus now and he were Cassius,
He should not humour me. I will this night

In several hands in at his windows throw,
As if they came from several citizens,
Writings all tending to the great opinion
That Rome holds of his name, wherein obscurely
Cæsar's ambition shall be glanced at.
And after this let Cæsar seat him sure,
For we will shake him, or worse days endure.

Exit.

scene 3.   [*A street*]

Thunder and lightning. Enter from opposite sides Casca, *with his sword drawn, and* Cicero

Cicero. Good even, Casca. Brought you Cæsar home?
  Why are you breathless, and why stare you so?

Casca. Are not you moved, when all the sway of earth
  Shakes like a thing unfirm? O Cicero,
  I have seen tempests, when the scolding winds
  Have rived the knotty oaks, and I have seen
  Th' ambitious ocean swell and rage and foam,
  To be exalted with the threatening clouds.
  But never till tonight, never till now,
  Did I go through a tempest dropping fire.
  Either there is a civil strife in heaven,
  Or else the world too saucy with the gods
  Incenses them to send destruction.

Cicero. Why, saw you any thing more wonderful?

Casca. A common slave—you know him well by sight—
  Held up his left hand, which did flame and burn
  Like twenty torches join'd, and yet his hand

Not sensible of fire remain'd unscorch'd.
Besides—I ha' not since put up my sword—
Against the Capitol I met a lion,
Who glazed upon me and went surly by
Without annoying me. And there were drawn
Upon a heap a hundred ghastly women
Transformed with their fear, who swore they saw
Men all in fire walk up and down the streets.
And yesterday the bird of night did sit
Even at noonday upon the market-place
Hooting and shrieking. When these prodigies
Do so conjointly meet, let not men say
'These are their reasons: they are natural.'
For I believe they are portentous things
Unto the climate that they point upon.

Cicero. Indeed, it is a strange-disposed time.
But men may construe things after their fashion
Clean from the purpose of the things themselves.
Comes Cæsar to the Capitol tomorrow?

Casca. He doth, for he did bid Antonius
Send word to you he would be there tomorrow.

Cicero. Good night then, Casca: this disturbed sky
Is not to walk in.

Casca.   Farewell, Cicero.

                                        Exit Cicero.

Enter Cassius

Cassius. Who's there?

Casca.   A Roman.

Cassius.   Casca, by your voice.

Casca. Your ear is good. Cassius, what night is this!

Cassius. A very pleasing night to honest men.

Casca. Who ever knew the heavens menace so?

Cassius. Those that have known the earth so full of faults.
    For my part, I have walk'd about the streets,
    Submitting me unto the perilous night,
    And thus unbraced, Casca, as you see,
    Have bared my bosom to the thunder-stone;
    And when the cross blue lightning seem'd to open
    The breast of heaven, I did present myself
    Even in the aim and very flash of it.

Casca. But wherefore did you so much tempt the heavens?
    It is the part of men to fear and tremble
    When the most mighty gods by tokens send
    Such dreadful heralds to astonish us.

Cassius. You are dull, Casca, and those sparks of life
    That should be in a Roman you do want,
    Or else you use not. You look pale and gaze
    And put on fear and cast yourself in wonder,
    To see the strange impatience of the heavens.
    But if you would consider the true cause
    Why all these fires, why all these gliding ghosts,
    Why birds and beasts from quality and kind,
    Why old men, fools, and children calculate,
    Why all these things change from their ordinance
    Their natures and preformed faculties
    To monstrous quality, why, you shall find
    That heaven hath infused them with these spirits
    To make them instruments of fear and warning
    Unto some monstrous state.
    Now could I, Casca, name to thee a man
    Most like this dreadful night,
    That thunders, lightens, opens graves, and roars

As doth the lion in the Capitol,
A man no mightier than thyself or me
In personal action, yet prodigious grown
And fearful, as these strange eruptions are.

Casca. 'Tis Cæsar that you mean. Is it not, Cassius?

Cassius. Let it be who it is: for Romans now
Have thews and limbs like to their ancestors;
But woe the while! Our fathers' minds are dead,
And we are govern'd with our mothers' spirits;
Our yoke and sufferance show us womanish.

Casca. Indeed they say the senators tomorrow
Mean to establish Cæsar as a king;
And he shall wear his crown by sea and land
In every place save here in Italy.

Cassius. I know where I will wear this dagger then:
Cassius from bondage will deliver Cassius.
Therein, ye gods, you make the weak most strong;
Therein, ye gods, you tyrants do defeat.
Nor stony tower, nor walls of beaten brass,
Nor airless dungeon, nor strong links of iron,
Can be retentive to the strength of spirit,
But life, being weary of these worldly bars,
Never lacks power to dismiss itself.
If I know this, know all the world besides,
That part of tyranny that I do bear
I can shake off at pleasure.

Thunder still.

Casca.   So can I.
So every bondman in his own hand bears
The power to cancel his captivity.

Cassius. And why should Cæsar be a tyrant then?
    Poor man! I know he would not be a wolf
    But that he sees the Romans are but sheep.
    He were no lion, were not Romans hinds.
    Those that with haste will make a mighty fire
    Begin it with weak straws. What trash is Rome?
    What rubbish and what offal, when it serves
    For the base matter to illuminate
    So vile a thing as Cæsar! But, O grief,
    Where hast thou led me? I perhaps speak this
    Before a willing bondman; then I know
    My answer must be made. But I am arm'd
    And dangers are to me indifferent.

Casca. You speak to Casca, and to such a man
    That is no fleering tell-tale. Hold, my hand:
    Be factious for redress of all these griefs,
    And I will set this foot of mine as far
    As who goes farthest.

Cassius.   There's a bargain made.
    Now know you, Casca, I have moved already
    Some certain of the noblest-minded Romans
    To undergo with me an enterprise
    Of honourable dangerous consequence;
    And I do know by this, they stay for me
    In Pompey's porch: for now, this fearful night,
    There is no stir or walking in the streets,
    And the complexion of the element
    In favour's like the work we have in hand,
    Most bloody, fiery, and most terrible.
                  Enter Cinna

Casca. Stand close awhile, for here comes one in haste.

Cassius. 'Tis Cinna; I do know him by his gait;
　He is a friend. Cinna, where haste you so?

Cinna. To find out you. Who's that? Metellus Cimber?

Cassius. No, it is Casca, one incorporate
　To our attempts. Am I not stay'd for, Cinna?

Cinna. I am glad on't. What a fearful night is this!
　There's two or three of us have seen strange sights.

Cassius. Am I not stay'd for? Tell me.

Cinna.　　　　　　　　　　　Yes, you are.
　O Cassius, if you could
　But win the noble Brutus to our party—

Cassius. Be you content. Good Cinna, take this paper
　And look you lay it in the prætors's chair,
　Where Brutus may but find it, and throw this
　In at his window. Set this up with wax
　Upon old Brutus' statue. All this done,
　Repair to Pompey's porch, where you shall find us.
　Is Decius Brutus and Trebonius there?

Cinna. All but Metellus Cimber, and he's gone
　To seek you at your house. Well, I will hie,
　And so bestow these papers as you bade me.

Cassius. That done, repair to Pompey's theatre.

　　　　　　　　　　　　　　　　　Exit Cinna.

　Come, Casca, you and I will yet ere day
　See Brutus at his house. Three parts of him
　Is ours already, and the man entire
　Upon the next encounter yields him ours.

Casca. O, he sits high in all the people's hearts.
　And that which would appear offence in us
　His countenance, like richest alchemy,
　Will change to virtue and to worthiness.

Cassius. Him and his worth and our great need of him
    You have right well conceited. Let us go,
    For it is after midnight, and ere day
    We will awake him and be sure of him.

                                Exeunt.

act 2

scene 1. [*Rome.* Brutus's *orchard*]

Enter Brutus

Brutus. What, Lucius, ho!
  I cannot by the progress of the stars
  Give guess how near to day. Lucius, I say!
  I would it were my fault to sleep so soundly.
  When, Lucius, when? Awake, I say! What, Lucius!
                    Enter Lucius

Lucius. Call'd you, my lord?

Brutus. Get me a taper in my study, Lucius.
  When it is lighted, come and call me here.

Lucius. I will, my lord.

                                    Exit.

Brutus. It must be by his death: and for my part
  I know no personal cause to spurn at him,
  But for the general. He would be crown'd:
  How that might change his nature, there's the question.
  It is the bright day that brings forth the adder;
  And that craves wary walking. Crown him—that—

And then, I grant, we put a sting in him
That at his will he may do danger with.
Th' abuse of greatness is when it disjoins
Remorse from power; and, to speak truth of Cæsar,
I have not known when his affections sway'd
More than his reason. But 'tis a common proof
That lowliness is young ambition's ladder,
Whereto the climber-upward turns his face;
But when he once attains the upmost round,
He then unto the ladder turns his back,
Looks in the clouds, scorning the base degrees
By which he did ascend: so Cæsar may.
Then, lest he may, prevent. And, since the quarrel
Will bear no colour for the thing he is,
Fashion it thus: that what he is, augmented,
Would run to these and these extremities.
And therefore think him as a serpent's egg,
Which hatch'd would as his kind grow mischievous,
And kill him in the shell.

Re-enter Lucius

Lucius. The taper burneth in your closet, sir.
　Searching the window for a flint, I found
　This paper thus seal'd up, and I am sure
　It did not lie there when I went to bed.

Gives him the letter.

Brutus. Get you to bed again; it is not day.
　Is not tomorrow, boy, the Ides of March?

Lucius. I know not, sir.

Brutus. Look in the calendar and bring me word.

Lucius. I will, sir.

Exit.

Brutus. The exhalations whizzing in the air
  Give so much light that I may read by them.

Opens the letter and reads.

> 'Brutus, thou sleep'st: awake and see thyself.
> Shall Rome, &c. Speak, strike, redress.
> Brutus, thou sleep'st: awake.'

Such instigations have been often dropp'd
Where I have took them up.
'Shall Rome, &c.' Thus must I piece it out:
Shall Rome stand under one man's awe? What Rome?
My ancestors did from the streets of Rome
The Tarquin drive, when he was call'd a king.
'Speak, strike, redress.' Am I entreated
To speak and strike? O Rome, I make thee promise,
If the redress will follow, thou receivest
Thy full petition at the hand of Brutus!

Re-enter Lucius

Lucius. Sir, March is wasted fifteen days.

Knocking within.

Brutus. 'Tis good. Go to the gate; somebody knocks.

Exit Lucius.

Since Cassius first did whet me against Cæsar
I have not slept.
Between the acting of a dreadful thing
And the first motion, all the interim is
Like a phantasma or a hideous dream:
The Genius and the mortal instruments
Are then in council, and the state of man,
Like to a little kingdom, suffers then
The nature of an insurrection.

Re-enter Lucius

Lucius. Sir, 'tis your brother Cassius at the door,
　Who doth desire to see you.

Brutus.　　　　　　　　　　Is he alone?

Lucius. No, sir, there are moe with him.

Brutus.　　　　　　　　　　Do you know them?

Lucius. No, sir, their hats are pluck'd about their ears
　And half their faces buried in their cloaks,
　That by no means I may discover them
　By any mark of favour.

Brutus.　　　　　　Let 'em enter.

　　　　　　　　　　　　　　　　Exit Lucius.

　They are the faction. O conspiracy,
　Sham'st thou to show thy dangerous brow by night,
　When evils are most free? O then by day
　Where wilt thou find a cavern dark enough
　To mask thy monstrous visage? Seek none, conspiracy:
　Hide it in smiles and affability,
　For if thou path, thy native semblance on,
　Not Erebus itself were dim enough
　To hide thee from prevention.

　　　　　　Enter the conspirators, Cassius, Casca, Decius,
　　　　　　　　Cinna, Metellus Cimber, *and* Trebonius

Cassius. I think we are too bold upon your rest:
　Good morrow, Brutus. Do we trouble you?

Brutus. I have been up this hour, awake all night.
　Know I these men that come along with you?

Cassius. Yes, every man of them; and no man here
　But honours you, and every one doth wish
　You had but that opinion of yourself
　Which every noble Roman bears of you.
　This is Trebonius.

Brutus.   He is welcome hither.

Cassius. This, Decius Brutus.

Brutus.   He is welcome too.

Cassius. This, Casca; this, Cinna; and this, Metellus Cimber.

Brutus. They are all welcome.
   What watchful cares do interpose themselves
   Betwixt your eyes and night?

Cassius. Shall I entreat a word?

                                    They whisper.

Decius. Here lies the east: doth not the day break here?

Casca. No.

Cinna. O, pardon, sir, it doth, and yon grey lines
   That fret the clouds are messengers of day.

Casca. You shall confess that you are both deceived.
   Here, as I point my sword, the sun arises,
   Which is a great way growing on the south,
   Weighing the youthful season of the year.
   Some two months hence up higher toward the north
   He first presents his fire, and the high east
   Stands as the Capitol, directly here.

Brutus. Give me your hands all over, one by one.

Cassius. And let us swear our resolution.

Brutus. No, not an oath. If not the face of men,
   The sufferance of our souls, the time's abuse—
   If these be motives weak, break off betimes,
   And every man hence to his idle bed.
   So let high-sighted tyranny range on
   Till each man drop by lottery. But if these,
   As I am sure they do, bear fire enough
   To kindle cowards and to steel with valour

The melting spirits of women, then, countrymen,
What need we any spur but our own cause
To prick us to redress? What other bond
Than secret Romans that have spoke the word,
And will not palter? And what other oath
Than honesty to honesty engaged
That this shall be or we will fall for it?
Swear priests and cowards and men cautelous,
Old feeble carrions and such suffering souls
That welcome wrongs: unto bad causes swear
Such creatures as men doubt. But do not stain
The even virtue of our enterprise,
Nor th' insuppressive mettle of our spirits,
To think that or our cause or our performance
Did need an oath, when every drop of blood
That every Roman bears, and nobly bears,
Is guilty of a several bastardy
If he do break the smallest particle
Of any promise that hath pass'd from him.

Cassius. But what of Cicero? Shall we sound him?
  I think he will stand very strong with us.

Casca. Let us not leave him out.

Cinna.   No, by no means.

Metellus. O let us have him, for his silver hairs
  Will purchase us a good opinion,
  And buy men's voices to commend our deeds.
  It shall be said his judgement ruled our hands.
  Our youths and wildness shall no whit appear,
  But all be buried in his gravity.

Brutus. O, name him not. Let us not break with him,
  For he will never follow any thing
  That other men begin.

Cassius.   Then leave him out.

Casca. Indeed he is not fit.

Decius. Shall no man else be touch'd but only Cæsar?

Cassius. Decius, well urged. I think it is not meet
   Mark Antony, so well beloved of Cæsar,
   Should outlive Cæsar. We shall find of him
   A shrewd contriver, and you know his means,
   If he improve them, may well stretch so far
   As to annoy us all, which to prevent
   Let Antony and Cæsar fall together.

Brutus. Our course will seem too bloody, Caius Cassius,
   To cut the head off and then hack the limbs,
   Like wrath in death and envy afterwards,
   For Antony is but a limb of Cæsar.
   Let us be sacrificers but not butchers, Caius.
   We all stand up against the spirit of Cæsar,
   And in the spirit of men there is no blood.
   O, that we then could come by Cæsar's spirit,
   And not dismember Cæsar! But, alas,
   Cæsar must bleed for it! And, gentle friends,
   Let's kill him boldly, but not wrathfully.
   Let's carve him as a dish fit for the gods,
   Not hew him as a carcass fit for hounds.
   And let our hearts, as subtle masters do,
   Stir up their servants to an act of rage
   And after seem to chide 'em. This shall make
   Our purpose necessary and not envious,
   Which so appearing to the common eyes,
   We shall be call'd purgers, not murderers.
   And for Mark Antony, think not of him,
   For he can do no more than Cæsar's arm
   When Cæsar's head is off.

Cassius.   Yet I fear him,
  For in the ingrafted love he bears to Cæsar—

Brutus. Alas, good Cassius, do not think of him.
  If he love Cæsar, all that he can do
  Is to himself, take thought and die for Cæsar.
  And that were much he should, for he is given
  To sports, to wildness and much company.

Trebonius. There is no fear in him. Let him not die,
  For he will live and laugh at this hereafter.

                                    Clock strikes.

Brutus. Peace! Count the clock.

Cassius.   The clock hath stricken three.

Trebonius. 'Tis time to part.

Cassius.   But it is doubtful yet
  Whether Cæsar will come forth today or no,
  For he is superstitious grown of late,
  Quite from the main opinion he held once
  Of fantasy, of dreams and ceremonies.
  It may be these apparent prodigies,
  The unaccustom'd terror of this night
  And the persuasion of his augurers,
  May hold him from the Capitol today.

Decius. Never fear that. If he be so resolved,
  I can o'ersway him; for he loves to hear
  That unicorns may be betray'd with trees
  And bears with glasses, elephants with holes,
  Lions with toils and men with flatterers:
  But when I tell him he hates flatterers,
  He says he does, being then most flattered.
  Let me work;
  For I can give his humour the true bent,
  And I will bring him to the Capitol.

Cassius. Nay, we will all of us be there to fetch him.

Brutus. By the eighth hour. Is that the uttermost?

Cinna. Be that the uttermost, and fail not then.

Metellus. Caius Ligarius doth bear Cæsar hard,
    Who rated him for speaking well of Pompey.
    I wonder none of you have thought of him.

Brutus. Now, good Metellus, go along by him.
    He loves me well, and I have given him reasons;
    Send him but hither, and I'll fashion him.

Cassius. The morning comes upon's. We'll leave you, Brutus:
    And, friends, disperse yourselves—but all remember
    What you have said and show yourselves true Romans.

Brutus. Good gentlemen, look fresh and merrily.
    Let not our looks put on our purposes,
    But bear it as our Roman actors do,
    With untired spirits and formal constancy.
    And so, good morrow to you every one.

                        Exeunt all but Brutus.

    Boy! Lucius! Fast asleep! It is no matter.
    Enjoy the honey-heavy dew of slumber.
    Thou hast no figures nor no fantasies,
    Which busy care draws in the brains of men;
    Therefore thou sleep'st so sound.

                  Enter Portia

Portia.   Brutus, my lord.

Brutus. Portia, what mean you? Wherefore rise you now?
    It is not for your health thus to commit
    Your weak condition to the raw cold morning.

Portia. Nor for yours neither. Y'have ungently, Brutus,
    Stole from my bed: and yesternight at supper
    You suddenly arose and walk'd about,

Musing and sighing, with your arms across;
And when I ask'd you what the matter was,
You stared upon me with ungentle looks.
I urged you further, then you scratch'd your head
And too impatiently stamp'd with your foot.
Yet I insisted, yet you answer'd not,
But with an angry wafture of your hand
Gave sign for me to leave you. So I did,
Fearing to strengthen that impatience
Which seem'd too much enkindled, and withal
Hoping it was but an effect of humour,
Which sometime hath his hour with every man.
It will not let you eat, nor talk, nor sleep,
And could it work so much upon your shape
As it hath much prevail'd on your condition,
I should not know you, Brutus. Dear my lord,
Make me acquainted with your cause of grief.

Brutus. I am not well in health, and that is all.

Portia. Brutus is wise, and were he not in health,
He would embrace the means to come by it.

Brutus. Why, so I do. Good Portia, go to bed.

Portia. Is Brutus sick, and is it physical
To walk unbraced and suck up the humours
Of the dank morning? What, is Brutus sick,
And will he steal out of his wholesome bed
To dare the vile contagion of the night,
And tempt the rheumy and unpurged air
To add unto his sickness? No, my Brutus,
You have some sick offence within your mind,
Which by the right and virtue of my place
I ought to know of: and upon my knees
I charm you, by my once commended beauty,

By all your vows of love and that great vow
Which did incorporate and make us one,
That you unfold to me, your self, your half,
Why you are heavy, and what men tonight
Have had resort to you; for here have been
Some six or seven, who did hide their faces
Even from darkness.

Brutus. Kneel not, gentle Portia.

Portia. I should not need, if you were gentle Brutus.
Within the bond of marriage, tell me, Brutus,
Is it excepted I should know no secrets
That appertain to you? Am I your self
But, as it were, in sort or limitation,
To keep with you at meals, comfort your bed,
And talk to you sometimes? Dwell I but in the suburbs
Of your good pleasure? If it be no more,
Portia is Brutus' harlot, not his wife.

Brutus. You are my true and honourable wife,
As dear to me as are the ruddy drops
That visit my sad heart.

Portia. If this were true, then should I know this secret.
I grant I am a woman, but withal
A woman that Lord Brutus took to wife.
I grant I am a woman, but withal
A woman well reputed, Cato's daughter.
Think you I am no stronger than my sex,
Being so father'd and so husbanded?
Tell me your counsels, I will not disclose 'em:
I have made strong proof of my constancy,
Giving myself a voluntary wound
Here in the thigh. Can I bear that with patience
And not my husband's secrets?

Brutus.   O ye gods,
  Render me worthy of this noble wife!

                                   Knocking within.

  Hark, hark, one knocks. Portia, go in a while,
  And by and by thy bosom shall partake
  The secrets of my heart.
  All my engagements I will construe to thee,
  All the charactery of my sad brows.
  Leave me with haste.

                                       Exit Portia.

  Lucius, who's that knocks?

                Re-enter Lucius *with* Ligarius

Lucius. Here is a sick man that would speak with you.

Brutus. Caius Ligarius, that Metellus spake of.
  Boy, stand aside. Caius Ligarius, how?

Ligarius. Vouchsafe good morrow from a feeble tongue.

Brutus. O, what a time have you chose out, brave Caius,
  To wear a kerchief. Would you were not sick!

Ligarius. I am not sick, if Brutus have in hand
  Any exploit worthy the name of honour.

Brutus. Such an exploit have I in hand, Ligarius,
  Had you a healthful ear to hear of it.

Ligarius. By all the gods that Romans bow before,
  I here discard my sickness. Soul of Rome!
  Brave son, derived from honourable loins,
  Thou, like an exorcist, hast conjured up
  My mortified spirit. Now bid me run
  And I will strive with things impossible,
  Yea, get the better of them. What's to do?

Brutus. A piece of work that will make sick men whole.

Ligarius. But are not some whole that we must make sick?

Brutus. That must we also. What it is, my Caius,
    I shall unfold to thee, as we are going
    To whom it must be done.

Ligarius.   Set on your foot,
    And with a heart new-fired I follow you,
    To do I know not what: but it sufficeth
    That Brutus leads me on.

Brutus.   Follow me then.

                                     Exeunt.

scene 2.   [Cæsar's *house*]

Thunder and lightning. Enter Cæsar, *in his night-gown*

Cæsar. Nor heaven nor earth have been at peace tonight:
    Thrice hath Calpurnia in her sleep cried out,
    'Help, ho! They murder Cæsar!' Who's within?

                  Enter a Servant

Servant. My lord?

Cæsar. Go bid the priests do present sacrifice
    And bring me their opinions of success.

Servant. I will, my lord.

                                       Exit.

                  Enter Calpurnia

Calpurnia. What mean you, Cæsar? Think you to walk forth?
    You shall not stir out of your house today.

Cæsar. Cæsar shall forth. The things that threaten'd me
    Ne'er look'd but on my back. When they shall see
    The face of Cæsar, they are vanished.

Calpurnia. Cæsar, I never stood on ceremonies,
    Yet now they fright me. There is one within,

Besides the things that we have heard and seen,
Recounts most horrid sights seen by the watch.
A lioness hath whelped in the streets,
And graves have yawn'd, and yielded up their dead.
Fierce fiery warriors fight upon the clouds
In ranks and squadrons and right form of war,
Which drizzled blood upon the Capitol.
The noise of battle hurtled in the air,
Horses did neigh and dying men did groan,
And ghosts did shriek and squeal about the streets.
O Cæsar! These things are beyond all use,
And I do fear them.

Cæsar.   What can be avoided
Whose end is purposed by the mighty gods?
Yet Cæsar shall go forth, for these predictions
Are to the world in general as to Cæsar.

Calpurnia. When beggars die there are no comets seen;
The heavens themselves blaze forth the death of princes.

Cæsar. Cowards die many times before their deaths;
The valiant never taste of death but once.
Of all the wonders that I yet have heard,
It seems to me most strange that men should fear,
Seeing that death, a necessary end,
Will come when it will come.
                    Re-enter Servant
                         What say the augurers?

Servant. They would not have you to stir forth today.
Plucking the entrails of an offering forth,
They could not find a heart within the beast.

Cæsar. The gods do this in shame of cowardice.
Cæsar should be a beast without a heart

If he should stay at home today for fear.
No, Cæsar shall not. Danger knows full well
That Cæsar is more dangerous than he.
We are two lions litter'd in one day,
And I the elder and more terrible:
And Cæsar shall go forth.

Calpurnia.   Alas, my lord,
Your wisdom is consumed in confidence.
Do not go forth today. Call it my fear
That keeps you in the house and not your own.
We'll send Mark Antony to the senate house,
And he shall say you are not well today:
Let me, upon my knee, prevail in this.

Cæsar. Mark Antony shall say I am not well,
And for thy humour I will stay at home.

                    Enter Decius

Here's Decius Brutus. He shall tell them so.

Decius. Cæsar, all hail! Good morrow, worthy Cæsar:
I come to fetch you to the senate house.

Cæsar. And you are come in very happy time
To bear my greeting to the senators
And tell them that I will not come today.
Cannot is false, and that I dare not, falser:
I will not come today: tell them so, Decius.

Calpurnia. Say he is sick.

Cæsar.   Shall Cæsar send a lie?
Have I in conquest stretch'd mine arm so far,
To be afeard to tell graybeards the truth?
Decius, go tell them Cæsar will not come.

Decius. Most mighty Cæsar, let me know some cause,
Lest I be laugh'd at when I tell them so.

Cæsar. The cause is in my will: I will not come.
   That is enough to satisfy the senate.
   But, for your private satisfaction,
   Because I love you, I will let you know.
   Calpurnia here, my wife, stays me at home.
   She dreamt tonight she saw my statue,
   Which like a fountain with an hundred spouts
   Did run pure blood, and many lusty Romans
   Came smiling and did bathe their hands in it.
   And these does she apply for warnings and portents
   And evils imminent, and on her knee
   Hath begg'd that I will stay at home today.

Decius. This dream is all amiss interpreted;
   It was a vision fair and fortunate.
   Your statue spouting blood in many pipes,
   In which so many smiling Romans bathed,
   Signifies that from you great Rome shall suck
   Reviving blood, and that great men shall press
   For tinctures, stains, relics and cognizance.
   This by Calpurnia's dream is signified.

Cæsar. And this way have you well expounded it.

Decius. I have, when you have heard what I can say.
   And know it now: the senate have concluded
   To give this day a crown to mighty Cæsar.
   If you shall send them word you will not come,
   Their minds may change. Besides, it were a mock
   Apt to be render'd, for some one to say
   'Break up the senate till another time,
   When Cæsar's wife shall meet with better dreams.'
   If Cæsar hide himself, shall they not whisper
   'Lo, Cæsar is afraid'?
   Pardon me, Cæsar, for my dear, dear love

To your proceeding bids me tell you this,
And reason to my love is liable.

Cæsar. How foolish do your fears seem now, Calpurnia!
I am ashamed I did yield to them.
Give me my robe, for I will go.

> *Enter* Publius, Brutus, Ligarius, Metellus, Casca,
> Trebonius, *and* Cinna

And look where Publius is come to fetch me.

Publius. Good morrow, Cæsar.

Cæsar.   Welcome, Publius.
What, Brutus, are you stirr'd so early too?
Good morrow, Casca. Caius Ligarius,
Cæsar was ne'er so much your enemy
As that same ague which hath made you lean.
What is 't o'clock?

Brutus.   Cæsar, 'tis strucken eight.

Cæsar. I thank you for your pains and courtesy.

> *Enter* Antony

See, Antony, that revels long o' nights,
Is notwithstanding up. Good morrow, Antony.

Antony. So to most noble Cæsar.

Cæsar.   Bid them prepare within.
I am to blame to be thus waited for.
Now, Cinna; now, Metellus; what, Trebonius!
I have an hour's talk in store for you.
Remember that you call on me today:
Be near me, that I may remember you.

Trebonius. Cæsar, I will. [*Aside*] And so near will I be,
That your best friends shall wish I had been further.

Cæsar. Good friends, go in and taste some wine with me;
And we like friends will straightway go together.

Brutus. [*Aside*] That every like is not the same, O Cæsar,
   The heart of Brutus yearns to think upon.

                                                    Exeunt.

scene 3.   [*A street near the Capitol*]

Enter Artemidorus, *reading a paper*

Artemidorus. 'Cæsar, beware of Brutus; take heed of Cassius; come not near Casca; have an eye to Cinna; trust not Trebonius; mark well Metellus Cimber: Decius Brutus loves thee not. Thou hast wronged Caius Ligarius. There is but one mind in all these men, and it is bent against Cæsar. If thou beest not immortal, look about you. Security gives way to conspiracy. The mighty gods defend thee!

                        Thy lover, ARTEMIDORUS.'

Here will I stand till Cæsar pass along,
   And as a suitor will I give him this.
   My heart laments that virtue cannot live
   Out of the teeth of emulation.
   If thou read this, O Cæsar, thou mayst live;
   If not, the Fates with traitors do contrive.

                                                    Exit.

scene 4.   [*Another part of the same street,
                before the house of Brutus*]

Enter Portia *and* Lucius

Portia. I prithee, boy, run to the senate house;
   Stay not to answer me, but get thee gone.
   Why dost thou stay?
Lucius.   To know my errand, madam.

Portia. I would have had thee there and here again,
    Ere I can tell thee what thou shouldst do there.
    [*Aside*] O constancy, be strong upon my side!
    Set a huge mountain 'tween my heart and tongue.
    I have a man's mind, but a woman's might.
    How hard it is for women to keep counsel!
    [*To Lucius*] Art thou here yet?

Lucius.   Madam, what should I do?
    Run to the Capitol, and nothing else?
    And so return to you, and nothing else?

Portia. Yes, bring me word, boy, if thy lord look well,
    For he went sickly forth. And take good note
    What Cæsar doth, what suitors press to him.
    Hark, boy, what noise is that?

Lucius. I hear none, madam.

Portia.   Prithee, listen well.
    I heard a bustling rumour like a fray,
    And the wind brings it from the Capitol.

Lucius. Sooth, madam, I hear nothing.

                Enter the Soothsayer

Portia.   Come hither, fellow:
    Which way hast thou been?

Soothsayer.   At mine own house, good lady.

Portia. What is 't o'clock?

Soothsayer.   About the ninth hour, lady.

Portia. Is Cæsar yet gone to the Capitol?

Soothsayer. Madam, not yet. I go to take my stand
    To see him pass on to the Capitol.

Portia. Thou hast some suit to Cæsar, hast thou not?

Soothsayer. That I have, lady, if it will please Cæsar
 To be so good to Cæsar as to hear me.
 I shall beseech him to befriend himself.

Portia. Why, know'st thou any harm's intended towards him?

Soothsayer. None that I know will be, much that I fear may
chance.
 Good morrow to you. Here the street is narrow.
 The throng that follows Cæsar at the heels,
 Of senators, of prætors, common suitors,
 Will crowd a feeble man almost to death.
 I'll get me to a place more void and there
 Speak to great Cæsar as he comes along.

Exit.

Portia. I must go in. Ay me, how weak a thing
 The heart of woman is. O Brutus,
 The heavens speed thee in thine enterprise!
 Sure the boy heard me. Brutus hath a suit
 That Cæsar will not grant. O, I grow faint.
 Run, Lucius, and commend me to my lord.
 Say I am merry. Come to me again,
 And bring me word what he doth say to thee.

Exeunt severally.

act 3

scene 1. [*Rome. Before the Capitol; the Senate sitting above*]

A crowd of people; among them Artemidorus *and the* Soothsayer.
Flourish. Enter Cæsar, Brutus, Cassius, Casca, Decius, Metellus,
Trebonius, Cinna, Antony, Lepidus, Popilius, Publius, *and others*

Cæsar. The Ides of March are come.

Soothsayer. Ay, Cæsar, but not gone.

Artemidorus. Hail, Cæsar! read this schedule.

Decius. Trebonius doth desire you to o'er-read,
   At your best leisure, this his humble suit.

Artemidorus. O Cæsar, read mine first, for mine's a suit
   That touches Cæsar nearer. Read it, great Cæsar.

Cæsar. What touches us ourself shall be last served.

Artemidorus. Delay not, Cæsar; read it instantly.

Cæsar. What, is the fellow mad?

Publius.   Sirrah, give place.

Cassius. What, urge you your petitions in the street?
   Come to the Capitol.

           Cæsar goes up to the senate house, the rest following.

Popilius. I wish your enterprise today may thrive.

Cassius. What enterprise, Popilius?

Popilius.   Fare you well.

Advances to Cæsar.

Brutus. What said Popilius Lena?

Cassius. He wish'd today our enterprise might thrive.
   I fear our purpose is discovered.

Brutus. Look how he makes to Cæsar. Mark him.

Cassius. Casca, be sudden, for we fear prevention.
   Brutus, what shall be done? If this be known,
   Cassius or Cæsar never shall turn back,
   For I will slay myself.

Brutus.   Cassius, be constant.
   Popilius Lena speaks not of our purposes,
   For, look, he smiles, and Cæsar doth not change.

Cassius. Trebonius knows his time; for look you, Brutus,
   He draws Mark Antony out of the way.

Exeunt Antony *and* Trebonius.

Decius. Where is Metellus Cimber? Let him go
   And presently prefer his suit to Cæsar.

Brutus. He is address'd: press near and second him.

Cinna. Casca, you are the first that rears your hand.

Cæsar. Are we all ready? What is now amiss
   That Cæsar and his senate must redress?

Metellus. Most high, most mighty and most puissant Cæsar,
   Metellus Cimber throws before thy seat
   An humble heart—

Kneeling.

Cæsar.   I must prevent thee, Cimber.
   These couchings and these lowly courtesies

Might fire the blood of ordinary men,
And turn pre-ordinance and first decree
Into the law of children. Be not fond
To think that Cæsar bears such rebel blood
That will be thaw'd from the true quality
With that which melteth fools—I mean sweet words,
Low-crooked court'sies and base spaniel fawning.
Thy brother by decree is banished:
If thou dost bend and pray and fawn for him,
I spurn thee like a cur out of my way.
Know, Cæsar doth not wrong, nor without cause
Will he be satisfied.

Metellus. Is there no voice more worthy than my own,
To sound more sweetly in great Cæsar's ear
For the repealing of my banish'd brother?

Brutus. I kiss thy hand, but not in flattery, Cæsar,
Desiring thee that Publius Cimber may
Have an immediate freedom of repeal.

Cæsar. What, Brutus!

Cassius.   Pardon, Cæsar; Cæsar, pardon:
As low as to thy foot doth Cassius fall
To beg enfranchisement for Publius Cimber.

Cæsar. I could be well moved, if I were as you;
If I could pray to move, prayers would move me.
But I am constant as the northern star,
Of whose true-fix'd and resting quality
There is no fellow in the firmament.
The skies are painted with unnumber'd sparks;
They are all fire and every one doth shine.
But there's but one in all doth hold his place.
So in the world: 'tis furnish'd well with men,
And men are flesh and blood, and apprehensive.

Yet in the number I do know but one
That unassailable holds on his rank,
Unshaked of motion. And that I am he,
Let me a little show it even in this,
That I was constant Cimber should be banish'd,
And constant do remain to keep him so.

Cinna. O Cæsar—

Cæsar.   Hence! Wilt thou lift up Olympus?

Decius. Great Cæsar—

Cæsar.   Doth not Brutus bootless kneel?

Casca. Speak hands for me!

> Casca *first, then the other Conspirators and*
> Marcus Brutus *stab* Cæsar.

Cæsar. Et tu, Brute? Then fall, Cæsar.

> *Dies.*

Cinna. Liberty! Freedom! Tyranny is dead!
Run hence, proclaim, cry it about the streets.

Cassius. Some to the common pulpits and cry out
'Liberty, freedom, and enfranchisement!'

Brutus. People and senators, be not affrighted.
Fly not; stand still: ambition's debt is paid.

Casca. Go to the pulpit, Brutus.

Decius. And Cassius too.

Brutus. Where's Publius?

Cinna. Here, quite confounded with this mutiny.

Metellus. Stand fast together, lest some friend of Cæsar's
Should chance—

Brutus. Talk not of standing. Publius, good cheer:
There is no harm intended to your person,
Nor to no Roman else. So tell them, Publius.

Cassius. And leave us, Publius, lest that the people
　Rushing on us should do your age some mischief.

Brutus. Do so, and let no man abide this deed
　But we the doers.

Re-enter Trebonius

Cassius. Where is Antony?

Trebonius. 　　　　　　Fled to his house amazed.
　Men, wives and children stare, cry out and run
　As it were doomsday.

Brutus. 　　　　　　Fates, we will know your pleasures.
　That we shall die, we know; 'tis but the time
　And drawing days out, that men stand upon.

Cassius. Why, he that cuts off twenty years of life
　Cuts off so many years of fearing death.

Brutus. Grant that, and then is death a benefit.
　So are we Cæsar's friends, that have abridged
　His time of fearing death. Stoop, Romans, stoop,
　And let us bathe our hands in Cæsar's blood
　Up to the elbows and besmear our swords.
　Then walk we forth, even to the market-place,
　And waving our red weapons o'er our heads
　Let's all cry 'Peace, freedom, and liberty!'

Cassius. Stoop then, and wash. How many ages hence
　Shall this our lofty scene be acted over
　In states unborn and accents yet unknown!

Brutus. How many times shall Cæsar bleed in sport,
　That now on Pompey's basis lies along
　No worthier than the dust!

Cassius. 　　　　　　　So oft as that shall be,
　So often shall the knot of us be call'd
　The men that gave their country liberty.

Decius. What, shall we forth?

Cassius.   Ay, every man away.
  Brutus shall lead, and we will grace his heels
  With the most boldest and best hearts of Rome.

                    Enter a Servant

Brutus. Soft! Who comes here? A friend of Antony's.

Servant. Thus, Brutus, did my master bid me kneel.
  Thus did Mark Antony bid me fall down,
  And being prostrate thus he bade me say:
  Brutus is noble, wise, valiant and honest;
  Cæsar was mighty, bold, royal and loving.
  Say I love Brutus and I honour him;
  Say I fear'd Cæsar, honour'd him and loved him.
  If Brutus will vouchsafe that Antony
  May safely come to him and be resolved
  How Cæsar hath deserved to lie in death,
  Mark Antony shall not love Cæsar dead
  So well as Brutus living, but will follow
  The fortunes and affairs of noble Brutus
  Thorough the hazards of this untrod state
  With all true faith. So says my master Antony.

Brutus. Thy master is a wise and valiant Roman;
  I never thought him worse.
  Tell him, so please him come unto this place,
  He shall be satisfied, and by my honour
  Depart untouch'd.

Servant.   I'll fetch him presently.

                                        Exit.

Brutus. I know that we shall have him well to friend.

Cassius. I wish we may, but yet have I a mind
  That fears him much, and my misgiving still
  Falls shrewdly to the purpose.

Enter Antony

Brutus. But here comes Antony. Welcome, Mark Antony.

Antony. O mighty Cæsar! Dost thou lie so low?
   Are all thy conquests, glories, triumphs, spoils,
   Shrunk to this little measure? Fare thee well.
   I know not, gentlemen, what you intend,
   Who else must be let blood, who else is rank.
   If I myself, there is no hour so fit
   As Cæsar's death's hour, nor no instrument
   Of half that worth as those your swords, made rich
   With the most noble blood of all this world.
   I do beseech ye, if you bear me hard,
   Now, whilst your purpled hands do reek and smoke,
   Fulfil your pleasure. Live a thousand years,
   I shall not find myself so apt to die.
   No place will please me so, no mean of death,
   As here by Cæsar, and by you cut off,
   The choice and master spirits of this age.

Brutus. O Antony, beg not your death of us.
   Though now we must appear bloody and cruel,
   As by our hands and this our present act
   You see we do, yet see you but our hands
   And this the bleeding business they have done:
   Our hearts you see not. They are pitiful,
   And pity to the general wrong of Rome—
   As fire drives out fire, so pity pity—
   Hath done this deed on Cæsar. For your part,
   To you our swords have leaden points, Mark Antony.
   Our arms in strength of malice, and our hearts
   Of brothers' temper, do receive you in
   With all kind love, good thoughts and reverence.

Cassius. Your voice shall be as strong as any man's
    In the disposing of new dignities.

Brutus. Only be patient till we have appeased
    The multitude, beside themselves with fear,
    And then we will deliver you the cause
    Why I, that did love Cæsar when I struck him,
    Have thus proceeded.

Antony.   I doubt not of your wisdom.
    Let each man render me his bloody hand.
    First, Marcus Brutus, will I shake with you;
    Next, Caius Cassius, do I take your hand;
    Now, Decius Brutus, yours; now yours, Metellus;
    Yours, Cinna; and, my valiant Casca, yours;
    Though last, not least in love, yours, good Trebonius.
    Gentlemen all—alas, what shall I say?
    My credit now stands on such slippery ground
    That one of two bad ways you must conceit me,
    Either a coward or a flatterer.
    That I did love thee, Cæsar, O 'tis true:
    If then thy spirit look upon us now,
    Shall it not grieve thee dearer than thy death
    To see thy Antony making his peace,
    Shaking the bloody fingers of thy foes?
    Most noble in the presence of thy corse,
    Had I as many eyes as thou hast wounds,
    Weeping as fast as they stream forth thy blood,
    It would become me better than to close
    In terms of friendship with thine enemies.
    Pardon me, Julius! Here wast thou bay'd, brave hart.
    Here didst thou fall, and here thy hunters stand,
    Sign'd in thy spoil and crimson'd in thy lethe.

O world, thou wast the forest to this hart,
And this indeed, O world, the heart of thee.
How like a deer strucken by many princes
Dost thou here lie!

Cassius. Mark Antony—

Antony. Pardon me, Caius Cassius.
The enemies of Cæsar shall say this;
Then, in a friend, it is cold modesty.

Cassius. I blame you not for praising Cæsar so;
But what compact mean you to have with us?
Will you be prick'd in number of our friends,
Or shall we on, and not depend on you?

Antony. Therefore I took your hands, but was indeed
Sway'd from the point by looking down on Cæsar.
Friends am I with you all, and love you all
Upon this hope, that you shall give me reasons
Why and wherein Cæsar was dangerous.

Brutus. Or else were this a savage spectacle.
Our reasons are so full of good regard
That were you, Antony, the son of Cæsar,
You should be satisfied.

Antony. That's all I seek,
And am moreover suitor that I may
Produce his body to the market-place,
And in the pulpit, as becomes a friend,
Speak in the order of his funeral.

Brutus. You shall, Mark Antony.

Cassius. Brutus, a word with you.
[*Aside to Brutus.*] You know not what you do. Do not consent
That Antony speak in his funeral.

Know you how much the people may be moved
By that which he will utter?

Brutus.   By your pardon:
I will myself into the pulpit first,
And show the reason of our Cæsar's death.
What Antony shall speak, I will protest
He speaks by leave and by permission,
And that we are contented Cæsar shall
Have all true rites and lawful ceremonies.
It shall advantage more than do us wrong.

Cassius. I know not what may fall; I like it not.

Brutus. Mark Antony, here, take you Cæsar's body.
You shall not in your funeral speech blame us,
But speak all good you can devise of Cæsar,
And say you do't by our permission,
Else shall you not have any hand at all
About his funeral. And you shall speak
In the same pulpit whereto I am going,
After my speech is ended.

Antony.   Be it so.
I do desire no more.

Brutus. Prepare the body then, and follow us.

                                   Exeunt all but Antony.

Antony. O pardon me, thou bleeding piece of earth,
That I am meek and gentle with these butchers!
Thou art the ruins of the noblest man
That ever lived in the tide of times.
Woe to the hand that shed this costly blood!
Over thy wounds now do I prophesy,
Which like dumb mouths do ope their ruby lips
To beg the voice and utterance of my tongue,

A curse shall light upon the limbs of men;
Domestic fury and fierce civil strife
Shall cumber all the parts of Italy;
Blood and destruction shall be so in use,
And dreadful objects so familiar,
That mothers shall but smile when they behold
Their infants quarter'd with the hands of war:
All pity choked with custom of fell deeds,
And Cæsar's spirit ranging for revenge
With Ate by his side come hot from hell,
Shall in these confines with a monarch's voice
Cry 'Havoc,' and let slip the dogs of war,
That this foul deed shall smell above the earth
With carrion men, groaning for burial.

Enter a Servant

You serve Octavius Cæsar, do you not?

Servant. I do, Mark Antony.

Antony. Cæsar did write for him to come to Rome.

Servant. He did receive his letters, and is coming,
And bid me say to you by word of mouth—
O Cæsar!

Seeing the body.

Antony. Thy heart is big; get thee apart and weep.
Passion, I see, is catching, for mine eyes,
Seeing those beads of sorrow stand in thine,
Begin to water. Is thy master coming?

Servant. He lies tonight within seven leagues of Rome.

Antony. Post back with speed and tell him what hath chanced.
Here is a mourning Rome, a dangerous Rome,
No Rome of safety for Octavius yet;
Hie hence, and tell him so. Yet stay awhile;

Thou shalt not back till I have borne this corse
Into the market-place. There shall I try
In my oration how the people take
The cruel issue of these bloody men,
According to the which thou shalt discourse
To young Octavius of the state of things.
Lend me your hand.

Exeunt with Cæsar's *body.*

scene 2. [*The Forum*]

Enter Brutus *and* Cassius, *and a throng of* Citizens

Citizens. We will be satisfied; let us be satisfied.

Brutus. Then follow me, and give me audience, friends.
Cassius, go you into the other street
And part the numbers.
Those that will hear me speak, let 'em stay here.
Those that will follow Cassius, go with him,
And public reasons shall be rendered
Of Cæsar's death.

First Citizen. I will hear Brutus speak.

Second Citizen. I will hear Cassius; and compare their reasons
When severally we hear them rendered.

Exit Cassius, *with some of the* Citizens.
Brutus *goes into the pulpit.*

Third Citizen. The noble Brutus is ascended: silence!

Brutus. Be patient till the last.
Romans, countrymen, and lovers, hear me for my cause and
be silent, that you may hear. Believe me for mine honour
and have respect to mine honour, that you may believe.

Censure me in your wisdom and awake your senses, that you may the better judge. If there be any in this assembly, any dear friend of Cæsar's, to him I say that Brutus' love to Cæsar was no less than his. If then that friend demand why Brutus rose against Cæsar, this is my answer: not that I loved Cæsar less, but that I loved Rome more. Had you rather Cæsar were living, and die all slaves, than that Cæsar were dead, to live all freemen? As Cæsar loved me, I weep for him; as he was fortunate, I rejoice at it; as he was valiant, I honour him; but as he was ambitious, I slew him. There is tears for his love; joy for his fortune; honour for his valour; and death for his ambition. Who is here so base that would be a bondman? If any, speak; for him have I offended. Who is here so rude that would not be a Roman? If any, speak, for him have I offended. Who is here so vile that will not love his country? If any, speak, for him have I offended. I pause for a reply.

All. None, Brutus, none.

Brutus. Then none have I offended. I have done no more to Cæsar than you shall do to Brutus. The question of his death is enrolled in the Capitol; his glory not extenuated, wherein he was worthy, nor his offences enforced, for which he suffered death.

       Enter Antony *and others, with* Cæsar's *body*

Here comes his body, mourned by Mark Antony, who, though he had no hand in his death, shall receive the benefit of his dying, a place in the commonwealth, as which of you shall not? With this I depart—that as I slew my best lover for the good of Rome, I have the same dagger for myself, when it shall please my country to need my death.

       Descends the pulpit.

All. Live, Brutus! Live, live!

First Citizen. Bring him with triumph home unto his house.

Second Citizen. Give him a statue with his ancestors.

Third Citizen. Let him be Cæsar.

Fourth Citizen.   Cæsar's better parts
 Shall be crown'd in Brutus.

First Citizen. We'll bring him to his house with shouts and
 clamours.

Brutus. My countrymen—

Second Citizen.   Peace! Silence! Brutus speaks.

First Citizen. Peace, ho!

Brutus. Good countrymen, let me depart alone,
 And, for my sake, stay here with Antony:
 Do grace to Cæsar's corpse, and grace his speech
 Tending to Cæsar's glories, which Mark Antony.
 By our permission is allow'd to make.
 I do entreat you, not a man depart,
 Save I alone, till Antony have spoke.

               Exit.

First Citizen. Stay, ho! And let us hear Mark Antony.

Third Citizen. Let him go up into the public chair.
 We'll hear him. Noble Antony, go up.

Antony. For Brutus' sake, I am beholding to you.

          Goes into the pulpit.

Fourth Citizen. What does he say of Brutus?

Third Citizen.   He says, for Brutus' sake,
 He finds himself beholding to us all.

Fourth Citizen. 'Twere best he speak no harm of Brutus here.

First Citizen. This Cæsar was a tyrant.

Third Citizen.   Nay, that's certain:
 We are blest that Rome is rid of him.

Second Citizen. Peace! Let us hear what Antony can say.

Antony. You gentle Romans—

All.   Peace, ho! Let us hear him.

Antony. Friends, Romans, countrymen, lend me your ears:
  I come to bury Cæsar, not to praise him.
  The evil that men do lives after them;
  The good is oft interred with their bones.
  So let it be with Cæsar. The noble Brutus
  Hath told you Cæsar was ambitious:
  If it were so, it was a grievous fault,
  And grievously hath Cæsar answer'd it.
  Here, under leave of Brutus and the rest—
  For Brutus is an honourable man;
  So are they all, all honourable men—
  Come I to speak in Cæsar's funeral.
  He was my friend, faithful and just to me;
  But Brutus says he was ambitious,
  And Brutus is an honourable man.
  He hath brought many captives home to Rome,
  Whose ransoms did the general coffers fill:
  Did this in Cæsar seem ambitious?
  When that the poor have cried, Cæsar hath wept:
  Ambition should be made of sterner stuff.
  Yet Brutus says he was ambitious,
  And Brutus is an honourable man.
  You all did see that on the Lupercal
  I thrice presented him a kingly crown,
  Which he did thrice refuse. Was this ambition?
  Yet Brutus says he was ambitious,
  And sure he is an honourable man.
  I speak not to disprove what Brutus spoke,
  But here I am to speak what I do know.

You all did love him once, not without cause:
What cause withholds you then to mourn for him?
O judgement! Thou art fled to brutish beasts
And men have lost their reason. Bear with me.
My heart is in the coffin there with Cæsar,
And I must pause till it come back to me.

First Citizen. Methinks there is much reason in his sayings.

Second Citizen. If thou consider rightly of the matter,
   Cæsar has had great wrong.

Third Citizen.   Has he, masters?
   I fear there will a worse come in his place.

Fourth Citizen. Mark'd ye his words? He would not take the
crown;
   Therefore 'tis certain he was not ambitious.

First Citizen. If it be found so, some will dear abide it.

Second Citizen. Poor soul, his eyes are red as fire with weeping.

Third Citizen. There's not a nobler man in Rome than Antony.

Fourth Citizen. Now mark him, he begins again to speak.

Antony. But yesterday the word of Cæsar might
   Have stood against the world. Now lies he there,
   And none so poor to do him reverence.
   O masters, if I were disposed to stir
   Your hearts and minds to mutiny and rage,
   I should do Brutus wrong and Cassius wrong,
   Who, you all know, are honourable men.
   I will not do them wrong. I rather choose
   To wrong the dead, to wrong myself and you,
   Than I will wrong such honourable men.
   But here's a parchment with the seal of Cæsar.
   I found it in his closet; 'tis his will.
   Let but the commons hear this testament—

Which, pardon me, I do not mean to read—
And they would go and kiss dead Cæsar's wounds
And dip their napkins in his sacred blood,
Yea, beg a hair of him for memory,
And, dying, mention it within their wills,
Bequeathing it as a rich legacy
Unto their issue.

Fourth Citizen. We'll hear the will: read it, Mark Antony.

All. The will, the will! We will hear Cæsar's will.

Antony. Have patience, gentle friends. I must not read it;
It is not meet you know how Cæsar loved you.
You are not wood, you are not stones, but men;
and being men, hearing the will of Cæsar,
It will inflame you, it will make you mad.
'Tis good you know not that you are his heirs,
For if you should, O, what would come of it!

Fourth Citizen. Read the will; we'll hear it, Antony.
You shall read us the will, Cæsar's will.

Antony. Will you be patient? Will you stay awhile?
I have o'ershot myself to tell you of it:
I fear I wrong the honourable men
Whose daggers have stabb'd Cæsar; I do fear it.

Fourth Citizen. They were traitors—honourable men!

All. The will! The testament!

Second Citizen. They were villains, murderers. The will! Read the will.

Antony. You will compel me then to read the will?
Then make a ring about the corpse of Cæsar,
And let me show you him that made the will.
Shall I descend? And will you give me leave?

All. Come down.

Second Citizen. Descend.

                            He comes down from the pulpit.

Third Citizen. You shall have leave.

Fourth Citizen. A ring; stand round.

First Citizen. Stand from the hearse, stand from the body.

Second Citizen. Room for Antony, most noble Antony.

Antony. Nay, press not so upon me. Stand far off.

All. Stand back. Room! Bear back.

Antony. If you have tears, prepare to shed them now.
   You all do know this mantle: I remember
   The first time ever Cæsar put it on.
   'Twas on a summer's evening, in his tent,
   That day he overcame the Nervii.
   Look, in this place ran Cassius' dagger through;
   See what a rent the envious Casca made;
   Through this the well-beloved Brutus stabb'd,
   And as he pluck'd his cursed steel away,
   Mark how the blood of Cæsar follow'd it,
   As rushing out of doors to be resolved
   If Brutus so unkindly knock'd or no:
   For Brutus, as you know, was Cæsar's angel.
   Judge, O you gods, how dearly Cæsar loved him!
   This was the most unkindest cut of all;
   For when the noble Cæsar saw him stab,
   Ingratitude, more strong than traitors' arms,
   Quite vanquish'd him. Then burst his mighty heart;
   And in his mantle muffling up his face,
   Even at the base of Pompey's statue,
   Which all the while ran blood, great Cæsar fell.

O what a fall was there, my countrymen!
Then I, and you, and all of us fell down,
Whilst bloody treason flourish'd over us.
O, now you weep, and I perceive you feel
The dint of pity: these are gracious drops.
Kind souls, what weep you when you but behold
Our Cæsar's vesture wounded? Look you here,
Here is himself, marr'd as you see with traitors.

First Citizen. O piteous spectacle!

Second Citizen. O noble Cæsar!

Third Citizen. O woeful day!

Fourth Citizen. O traitors, villains!

First Citizen. O most bloody sight!

Second Citizen. We will be revenged.

All. Revenge! About! Seek! Burn! Fire! Kill!
Slay! Let not a traitor live!

Antony. Stay, countrymen.

First Citizen. Peace there! Hear the noble Antony.

Second Citizen. We'll hear him, we'll follow him, we'll die with him.

Antony. Good friends, sweet friends, let me not stir you up
To such a sudden flood of mutiny.
They that have done this deed are honourable;
What private griefs they have, alas, I know not,
That made them do it: they are wise and honourable
And will, no doubt, with reasons answer you.
I come not, friends, to steal away your hearts.
I am no orator, as Brutus is,
But, as you know me all, a plain blunt man

That love my friend, and that they know full well
That gave me public leave to speak of him.
For I have neither wit, nor words, nor worth,
Action, nor utterance, nor the power of speech
To stir men's blood. I only speak right on:
I tell you that which you yourselves do know,
Show you sweet Cæsar's wounds, poor poor dumb mouths,
And bid them speak for me. But were I Brutus,
And Brutus Antony, there were an Antony
Would ruffle up your spirits and put a tongue
In every wound of Cæsar, that should move
The stones of Rome to rise and mutiny.

All. We'll mutiny.

First Citizen. We'll burn the house of Brutus.

Third Citizen. Away, then! Come, seek the conspirators.

Antony. Yet hear me, countrymen, yet hear me speak.

All. Peace, ho! Hear Antony. Most noble Antony!

Antony. Why, friends, you go to do you know not what.
    Wherein hath Cæsar thus deserved your loves?
    Alas, you know not; I must tell you then.
    You have forgot the will I told you of.

All. Most true: the will! Let's stay and hear the will.

Antony. Here is the will, and under Cæsar's seal.
    To every Roman citizen he gives,
    To every several man, seventy five drachmas.

Second Citizen. Most noble Cæsar! We'll revenge his death.

Third Citizen. O royal Cæsar!

Antony. Hear me with patience.

All. Peace, ho!

Antony. Moreover, he hath left you all his walks,
    His private arbours and new-planted orchards,
    On this side Tiber. He hath left them you
    And to your heirs for ever: common pleasures
    To walk abroad and recreate yourselves.
    Here was a Cæsar! When comes such another?

First Citizen. Never, never. Come, away, away!
    We'll burn his body in the holy place,
    And with the brands fire the traitors' houses.
    Take up the body.

Second Citizen. Go fetch fire.

Third Citizen. Pluck down benches.

Fourth Citizen. Pluck down forms, windows, any thing.
                              Exeunt Citizens *with the body.*

Antony. Now let it work. Mischief, thou art afoot,
    Take thou what course thou wilt.
                  Enter a Servant
                      How now, fellow?

Servant. Sir, Octavius is already come to Rome.

Antony. Where is he?

Servant. He and Lepidus are at Cæsar's house.

Antony. And thither will I straight to visit him.
    He comes upon a wish. Fortune is merry,
    And in this mood will give us any thing.

Servant. I heard him say Brutus and Cassius
    Are rid like madmen through the gates of Rome.

Antony. Belike they had some notice of the people,
    How I had moved them. Bring me to Octavius.
                                   Exeunt.

scene 3. [*A street*]

Enter Cinna *the poet*

Cinna. I dreamt tonight that I did feast with Cæsar,
And things unluckily charge my fantasy,
I have no will to wander forth of doors,
Yet something leads me forth.

Enter Citizens

First Citizen. What is your name?

Second Citizen. Whither are you going?

Third Citizen. Where do you dwell?

Fourth Citizen. Are you a married man or a bachelor?

Second Citizen. Answer every man directly.

First Citizen. Ay, and briefly.

Fourth Citizen. Ay, and wisely.

Third Citizen. Ay, and truly, you were best.

Cinna. What is my name? Whither am I going?
Where do I dwell? Am I a married man or a bachelor?
Then, to answer every man directly and briefly, wisely and
truly: wisely I say, I am a bachelor.

Second Citizen. That's as much as to say, they are fools that
marry. You'll bear me a bang for that, I fear.
Proceed, directly.

Cinna. Directly, I am going to Cæsar's funeral.

First Citizen. As a friend or an enemy?

Cinna. As a friend.

Second Citizen. That matter is answered directly.

Fourth Citizen. For your dwelling, briefly.

Cinna. Briefly, I dwell by the Capitol.

Third Citizen. Your name, sir, truly.

Cinna. Truly, my name is Cinna.

First Citizen. Tear him to pieces; he's a conspirator.

Cinna. I am Cinna the poet, I am Cinna the poet.

Fourth Citizen. Tear him for his bad verses, tear him for his bad verses.

Cinna. I am not Cinna the conspirator.

Fourth Citizen. It is no matter, his name's Cinna. Pluck but his name out of his heart and turn him going.

Third Citizen. Tear him, tear him! Come, brands, ho! Firebrands: to Brutus', to Cassius', burn all! Some to Decius' house, and some to Casca's; some to Ligarius'—away, go!

Exeunt.

act 4

scene 1. [*A house in Rome*]

Enter Antony, Octavius, *and* Lepidus

Antony. These many then shall die; their names are prick'd.

Octavius. Your brother too must die; consent you, Lepidus?

Lepidus. I do consent—

Octavius.　　　　　Prick him down, Antony.

Lepidus. Upon condition Publius shall not live,
Who is your sister's son, Mark Antony.

Antony. He shall not live. Look, with a spot I damn him.
But, Lepidus, go you to Cæsar's house;
Fetch the will hither, and we shall determine
How to cut off some charge in legacies.

Lepidus. What, shall I find you here?

Octavius. Or here, or at the Capitol.

　　　　　　　　　　　　　　　　Exit Lepidus.

Antony. This is a slight unmeritable man,
Meet to be sent on errands: is it fit,

The three-fold world divided, he should stand
One of the three to share it?

Octavius.   So you thought him,
And took his voice who should be prick'd to die
In our black sentence and proscription.

Antony. Octavius, I have seen more days than you,
And though we lay these honours on this man,
To ease ourselves of divers slanderous loads,
He shall but bear them as the ass bears gold,
To groan and sweat under the business,
Either led or driven, as we point the way;
And having brought our treasure where we will,
Then take we down his load and turn him off,
Like to the empty ass, to shake his ears
And graze in commons.

Octavius.   You may do your will,
But he's a tried and valiant soldier.

Antony. So is my horse, Octavius, and for that
I do appoint him store of provender:
It is a creature that I teach to fight,
To wind, to stop, to run directly on,
His corporal motion govern'd by my spirit.
And, in some taste, is Lepidus but so.
He must be taught, and train'd, and bid go forth;
A barren-spirited fellow; one that feeds
On objects, arts and imitations,
Which, out of use and staled by other men,
Begin his fashion. Do not talk of him
But as a property. And now, Octavius,
Listen great things. Brutus and Cassius
Are levying powers: we must straight make head.
Therefore let our alliance be combined,

Our best friends made, our means stretch'd,
And let us presently go sit in council,
How covert matters may be best disclosed,
And open perils surest answered.

Octavius. Let us do so: for we are at the stake
And bay'd about with many enemies,
And some that smile have in their hearts, I fear,
Millions of mischiefs.

                                         Exeunt.

scene 2.   [*Camp near Sardis; Before* Brutus's *tent*]

    Drum. Enter Brutus, Lucilius, Lucius, *and* Soldiers;
            Titinius *and* Pindarus *meet them*

Brutus. Stand ho!

Lucilius. Give the word, ho, and stand.

Brutus. What now, Lucilius, is Cassius near?

Lucilius. He is at hand, and Pindarus is come
To do you salutation from his master.

Brutus. He greets me well. Your master, Pindarus,
In his own change, or by ill officers,
Hath given me some worthy cause to wish
Things done, undone: but if he be at hand,
I shall be satisfied.

Pindarus.   I do not doubt
But that my noble master will appear
Such as he is, full of regard and honour.

Brutus. He is not doubted. A word, Lucilius,
How he received you: let me be resolved.

Lucilius. With courtesy and with respect enough,

But not with such familiar instances
Nor with such free and friendly conference
As he hath used of old.

Brutus.   Thou hast described
A hot friend cooling. Ever note, Lucilius,
When love begins to sicken and decay,
It useth an enforced ceremony.
There are no tricks in plain and simple faith:
But hollow men, like horses hot at hand,
Make gallant show and promise of their mettle,
But when they should endure the bloody spur,
They fall their crests and like deceitful jades
Sink in the trial. Comes his army on?

Lucilius. They mean this night in Sardis to be quarter'd.
The greater part, the horse in general,
Are come with Cassius.

> *Low march within.*

Brutus.   Hark! He is arrived:
March gently on to meet him.

> *Enter* Cassius *and his powers*

Cassius. Stand, ho!

Brutus. Stand, ho! Speak the word along.

First Soldier. Stand!

Second Soldier. Stand!

Third Soldier. Stand!

Cassius. Most noble brother, you have done me wrong.

Brutus. Judge me, you gods! Wrong I mine enemies?
And if not so, how should I wrong a brother?

Cassius. Brutus, this sober form of yours hides wrongs,
And when you do them—

Brutus. Cassius, be content.
 Speak your griefs softly: I do know you well.
 Before the eyes of both our armies here,
 Which should perceive nothing but love from us,
 Let us not wrangle. Bid them move away,
 Then in my tent, Cassius, enlarge your griefs
 And I will give you audience.

Cassius. Pindarus,
 Bid our commanders lead their charges off
 A little from this ground.

Brutus. Lucilius, do you the like, and let no man
 Come to our tent till we have done our conference.
 Let Lucius and Titinius guard our door.

             Exeunt.

scene 3. [Brutus's *tent*]

Enter Brutus *and* Cassius

Cassius. That you have wrong'd me doth appear in this:
 You have condemn'd and noted Lucius Pella
 For taking bribes here of the Sardians;
 Wherein my letters, praying on his side
 Because I knew the man, were slighted off.

Brutus. You wrong'd yourself to write in such a case.

Cassius. In such a time as this it is not meet
 That every nice offence should bear his comment.

Brutus. Let me tell you, Cassius, you yourself
 Are much condemn'd to have an itching palm,
 To sell and mart your offices for gold
 To undeservers.

Cassius.　　　　I, an itching palm!
　You know that you are Brutus that speaks this,
　Or, by the gods, this speech were else your last.

Brutus. The name of Cassius honours this corruption,
　And chastisement doth therefore hide his head.

Cassius. Chastisement!

Brutus. Remember March, the Ides of March remember:
　Did not great Julius bleed for justice' sake?
　What villain touch'd his body, that did stab
　And not for justice? What, shall one of us,
　That struck the foremost man of all this world
　But for supporting robbers, shall we now
　Contaminate our fingers with base bribes,
　And sell the mighty space of our large honours
　For so much trash as may be grasped thus?
　I had rather be a dog and bay the moon
　Than such a Roman.

Cassius.　　　　Brutus, bait not me.
　I'll not endure it. You forget yourself
　To hedge me in. I am a soldier, I,
　Older in practice, abler than yourself
　To make conditions.

Brutus.　　　　Go to; you are not, Cassius.

Cassius. I am.

Brutus. I say you are not.

Cassius. Urge me no more, I shall forget myself.
　Have mind upon your health; tempt me no farther.

Brutus. Away, slight man!

Cassius. Is't possible?

Brutus.　　　　Hear me, for I will speak.

Must I give way and room to your rash choler?
Shall I be frighted when a madman stares?

Cassius. O ye gods, ye gods! Must I endure all this?

Brutus. All this! Ay, more: fret till your proud heart break.
Go show your slaves how choleric you are,
And make your bondmen tremble. Must I budge?
Must I observe you? Must I stand and crouch
Under your testy humour? By the gods,
You shall digest the venom of your spleen,
Though it do split you; for, from this day forth,
I'll use you for my mirth, yea, for my laughter,
When you are waspish.

Cassius. Is it come to this?

Brutus. You say you are a better soldier:
Let it appear so. Make your vaunting true
And it shall please me well. For mine own part,
I shall be glad to learn of noble men.

Cassius. You wrong me every way; you wrong me, Brutus.
I said an elder soldier, not a better.
Did I say better?

Brutus. If you did, I care not.

Cassius. When Cæsar lived, he durst not thus have moved me.

Brutus. Peace, peace! You durst not so have tempted him.

Cassius. I durst not?

Brutus. No.

Cassius. What, durst not tempt him!

Brutus. For your life you durst not.

Cassius. Do not presume too much upon my love;
I may do that I shall be sorry for.

Brutus. You have done that you should be sorry for.
    There is no terror, Cassius, in your threats,
    For I am arm'd so strong in honesty
    That they pass by me as the idle wind
    Which I respect not. I did send to you
    For certain sums of gold, which you denied me,
    For I can raise no money by vile means:
    By heaven, I had rather coin my heart
    And drop my blood for drachmas, than to wring
    From the hard hands of peasants their vile trash
    By any indirection. I did send
    To you for gold to pay my legions,
    Which you denied me: was that done like Cassius?
    Should I have answer'd Caius Cassius so?
    When Marcus Brutus grows so covetous,
    To lock such rascal counters from his friends,
    Be ready, gods, with all your thunderbolts
    Dash him to pieces!

Cassius.   I denied you not.

Brutus. You did.

Cassius.   I did not. He was but a fool
    That brought my answer back. Brutus hath rived my heart:
    A friend should bear his friend's infirmities,
    But Brutus makes mine greater than they are.

Brutus. I do not, till you practise them on me.

Cassius. You love me not.

Brutus.   I do not like your faults.

Cassius. A friendly eye could never see such faults.

Brutus. A flatterer's would not, though they do appear
    As huge as high Olympus.

Cassius. Come, Antony, and young Octavius, come,
　Revenge yourselves alone on Cassius,
　For Cassius is aweary of the world:
　Hated by one he loves; braved by his brother;
　Check'd like a bondman; all his faults observed,
　Set in a note-book, learn'd and conn'd by rote,
　To cast into my teeth. O, I could weep
　My spirit from mine eyes! There is my dagger
　And here my naked breast: within, a heart
　Dearer than Plutus' mine, richer than gold.
　If that thou be'st a Roman, take it forth;
　I, that denied thee gold, will give my heart.
　Strike, as thou didst at Cæsar, for I know,
　When thou didst hate him worst, thou lovedst him better
　Than ever thou lovedst Cassius.

Brutus.　　　　　　　　　Sheathe your dagger:
　Be angry when you will, it shall have scope;
　Do what you will, dishonour shall be humour.
　O Cassius, you are yoked with a lamb
　That carries anger as the flint bears fire,
　Who, much enforced, shows a hasty spark
　And straight is cold again.

Cassius.　　　　　　　　Hath Cassius lived
　To be but mirth and laughter to his Brutus,
　When grief and blood ill-temper'd vexeth him?

Brutus. When I spoke that, I was ill-temper'd too.

Cassius. Do you confess so much? Give me your hand.

Brutus. And my heart too.

Cassius.　　　　　　O Brutus!

Brutus.　　　　　　　　　What's the matter?

Cassius. Have not you love enough to bear with me,
    When that rash humour which my mother gave me
    Makes me forgetful?

Brutus.   Yes, Cassius, and from henceforth
    When you are over-earnest with your Brutus,
    He'll think your mother chides, and leave you so.

Poet. [*Within*] Let me go in to see the generals.
    There is some grudge between 'em; 'tis not meet
    They be alone.

Lucilius. [*Within*] You shall not come to them.

Poet. [*Within*] Nothing but death shall stay me.
        Enter Poet, *followed by* Lucilius, Titinius, *and* Lucius

Cassius. How now! What's the matter?

Poet. For shame, you generals! What do you mean?
    Love, and be friends, as two such men should be,
    For I have seen more years, I'm sure, than ye.

Cassius. Ha, ha, how vilely doth this cynic rhyme!

Brutus. Get you hence, sirrah; saucy fellow, hence!

Cassius. Bear with him, Brutus, 'tis his fashion.

Brutus. I'll know his humour when he knows his time:
    What should the wars do with these jigging fools?
    Companion, hence!

Cassius.   Away, away, be gone!
                                        Exit Poet.

Brutus. Lucilius and Titinius, bid the commanders
    Prepare to lodge their companies tonight.

Cassius. And come yourselves, and bring Messala with you
    Immediately to us.
                        Exeunt Lucilius *and* Titinius.

Brutus.   Lucius, a bowl of wine!

                                     Exit Lucius.

Cassius. I did not think you could have been so angry.

Brutus. O Cassius, I am sick of many griefs.

Cassius. Of your philosophy you make no use,
    If you give place to accidental evils.

Brutus. No man bears sorrow better: Portia is dead.

Cassius. Ha? Portia!

Brutus. She is dead.

Cassius. How 'scaped I killing when I cross'd you so?
    O insupportable and touching loss!
    Upon what sickness?

Brutus.   Impatient of my absence,
    And grief that young Octavius with Mark Antony
    Have made themselves so strong—for with her death
    That tidings came—with this she fell distract,
    And, her attendants absent, swallow'd fire.

Cassius. And died so?

Brutus.   Even so.

Cassius.   O ye immortal gods!

           Re-enter Lucius, *with wine and taper*

Brutus. Speak no more of her. Give me a bowl of wine.
    In this I bury all unkindness, Cassius.

                                     Drinks.

Cassius. My heart is thirsty for that noble pledge.
    Fill, Lucius, till the wine o'erswell the cup.
    I cannot drink too much of Brutus' love.

                                     Drinks.

Brutus. Come in, Titinius!

                                  Exit Lucius.

Re-enter Titinius, *with* Messala

              Welcome, good Messala.
Now sit we close about this taper here
And call in question our necessities.

Cassius. Portia, art thou gone?

Brutus.   No more, I pray you.
Messala, I have here received letters
That young Octavius and Mark Antony
Come down upon us with a mighty power,
Bending their expedition toward Philippi.

Messala. Myself have letters of the selfsame tenour.

Brutus. With what addition?

Messala. That by proscription and bills of outlawry
Octavius, Antony, and Lepidus
Have put to death an hundred senators.

Brutus. Therein our letters do not well agree;
Mine speak of seventy senators that died
By their proscriptions, Cicero being one.

Cassius. Cicero one!

Messala.   Cicero is dead,
And by that order of proscription.
Had you your letters from your wife, my lord?

Brutus. No, Messala.

Messala. Nor nothing in your letters writ of her?

Brutus. Nothing, Messala.

Messala.   That, methinks, is strange.

Brutus. Why ask you? Hear you aught of her in yours?

Messala. No, my lord.

Brutus. Now, as you are a Roman, tell me true.

Messala. Then like a Roman bear the truth I tell,
    For certain she is dead, and by strange manner.

Brutus. Why, farewell, Portia. We must die, Messala:
    With meditating that she must die once
    I have the patience to endure it now.

Messala. Even so great men great losses should endure.

Cassius. I have as much of this in art as you,
    But yet my nature could not bear it so.

Brutus. Well, to our work alive. What do you think
    Of marching to Philippi presently?

Cassius. I do not think it good.

Brutus.   Your reason?

Cassius.   This it is:
    'Tis better that the enemy seek us,
    So shall he waste his means, weary his soldiers,
    Doing himself offence, whilst we lying still
    Are full of rest, defence and nimbleness.

Brutus. Good reasons must of force give place to better.
    The people 'twixt Philippi and this ground
    Do stand but in a forced affection,
    For they have grudged us contribution.
    The enemy, marching along by them,
    By them shall make a fuller number up,
    Come on refresh'd, new-added and encouraged;
    From which advantage shall we cut him off
    If at Philippi we do face him there,
    These people at our back.

Cassius.   Hear me, good brother.

Brutus. Under your pardon. You must note beside
    That we have tried the utmost of our friends,

Our legions are brim-full, our cause is ripe.
The enemy increaseth every day;
We, at the height, are ready to decline.
There is a tide in the affairs of men
Which taken at the flood leads on to fortune;
Omitted, all the voyage of their life
Is bound in shallows and in miseries.
On such a full sea are we now afloat,
And we must take the current when it serves,
Or lose our ventures.

Cassius. Then with your will go on;
We'll along ourselves and meet them at Philippi.

Brutus. The deep of night is crept upon our talk,
And nature must obey necessity;
Which we will niggard with a little rest.
There is no more to say.

Cassius. No more. Good night.
Early tomorrow will we rise and hence.

Brutus. Lucius!

Re-enter Lucius

My gown.

Exit Lucius.

Farewell, good Messala;
Good night, Titinius. Noble, noble Cassius,
Good night, and good repose.

Cassius. O my dear brother,
This was an ill beginning of the night:
Never come such division 'tween our souls!
Let it not, Brutus.

Brutus. Everything is well.

Cassius. Good night, my lord.

Brutus.   Good night, good brother.

Titinius. Messala. Good night, Lord Brutus.

Brutus.   Farewell, every one.

> *Exeunt all but* Brutus.

> *Re-enter* Lucius, *with the gown*

Give me the gown. Where is thy instrument?

Lucius. Here in the tent.

Brutus.   What, thou speak'st drowsily?
   Poor knave, I blame thee not; thou art o'er-watch'd.
   Call Claudius and some other of my men;
   I'll have them sleep on cushions in my tent.

Lucius. Varro and Claudius!

> *Enter* Varro *and* Claudius

Varro. Calls my lord?

Brutus. I pray you, sirs, lie in my tent and sleep.
   It may be I shall raise you by and by
   On business to my brother Cassius.

Varro. So please you, we will stand and watch your pleasure.

Brutus. I will not have it so: lie down, good sirs.
   It may be I shall otherwise bethink me.
   Look, Lucius, here's the book I sought for so;
   I put it in the pocket of my gown.

> Varro *and* Claudius *lie down.*

Lucius. I was sure your lordship did not give it me.

Brutus. Bear with me, good boy, I am much forgetful.
   Canst thou hold up thy heavy eyes awhile,
   And touch thy instrument a strain or two?

Lucius. Ay, my lord, an't please you.

Brutus.   It does, my boy.
   I trouble thee too much, but thou art willing.

Lucius. It is my duty, sir.

Brutus. I should not urge thy duty past thy might;
    I know young bloods look for a time of rest.

Lucius. I have slept, my lord, already.

Brutus. It was well done, and thou shalt sleep again.
    I will not hold thee long: if I do live,
    I will be good to thee.

Music, and a song.

This is a sleepy tune. O murderous slumber,
Lay'st thou thy leaden mace upon my boy,
That plays thee music? Gentle knave, good night;
I will not do thee so much wrong to wake thee.
If thou dost nod, thou break'st thy instrument;
I'll take it from thee; and, good boy, good night.
Let me see, let me see: is not the leaf turn'd down
Where I left reading? Here it is, I think.

Sits down.

Enter the Ghost of Cæsar

How ill this taper burns. Ha! Who comes here?
I think it is the weakness of mine eyes
That shapes this monstrous apparition.
It comes upon me. Art thou any thing?
Art thou some god, some angel, or some devil,
That makest my blood cold, and my hair to stare?
Speak to me what thou art.

Ghost. Thy evil spirit, Brutus.

Brutus.   Why comest thou?

Ghost. To tell thee thou shalt see me at Philippi.

Brutus. Well; then I shall see thee again?

Ghost. Ay, at Philippi.

Brutus. Why, I will see thee at Philippi then.

Exit Ghost.

Now I have taken heart thou vanishest.
Ill spirit, I would hold more talk with thee.
Boy, Lucius! Varro! Claudius! Sirs, awake!
Claudius!

Lucius. The strings, my lord, are false.

Brutus. He thinks he still is at his instrument.
Lucius, awake!

Lucius. My lord?

Brutus. Didst thou dream, Lucius, that thou so criedst out?

Lucius. My lord, I do not know that I did cry.

Brutus. Yes, that thou didst: didst thou see any thing?

Lucius. Nothing, my lord.

Brutus. Sleep again, Lucius. Sirrah Claudius!
[*To Varro*] Fellow thou, awake!

Varro. My lord?

Claudius. My lord?

Brutus. Why did you so cry out, sirs, in your sleep?

Varro. Claudius. Did we, my lord?

Brutus.   Ay. Saw you any thing?

Varro. No, my lord, I saw nothing.

Claudius.   Nor I, my lord.

Brutus. Go and commend me to my brother Cassius.
Bid him set on his powers betimes before,
And we will follow.

Varro. Claudius.   It shall be done, my lord.

Exeunt.

act 5

scene 1. [*The plains of Philippi*]

Enter Octavius, Antony, *and their army*

Octavius. Now, Antony, our hopes are answered:
You said the enemy would not come down,
But keep the hills and upper regions.
It proves not so: their battles are at hand.
They mean to warn us at Philippi here,
Answering before we do demand of them.

Antony. Tut, I am in their bosoms, and I know
Wherefore they do it: they could be content
To visit other places and come down
With fearful bravery, thinking by this face
To fasten in our thoughts that they have courage.
But 'tis not so.

Enter a Messenger

Messenger.   Prepare you, generals:
The enemy comes on in gallant show.
Their bloody sign of battle is hung out,
And something to be done immediately.

Antony. Octavius, lead your battle softly on,
   Upon the left hand of the even field.

Octavius. Upon the right hand I; keep thou the left.

Antony. Why do you cross me in this exigent?

Octavius. I do not cross you, but I will do so.

                                             March.

   Drum. Enter Brutus, Cassius, *and their army*; Lucilius,
              Titinius, Messala *and others*

Brutus. They stand, and would have parley.

Cassius. Stand fast, Titinius. We must out and talk.

Octavius. Mark Antony, shall we give sign of battle?

Antony. No, Cæsar, we will answer on their charge.
   Make forth; the generals would have some words.

Octavius. Stir not until the signal.

Brutus. Words before blows: is it so, countrymen?

Octavius. Not that we love words better, as you do.

Brutus. Good words are better than bad strokes, Octavius.

Antony. In your bad strokes, Brutus, you give good words:
   Witness the hole you made in Cæsar's heart,
   Crying 'Long live! Hail, Cæsar!'

Cassius.   Antony,
   The posture of your blows are yet unknown;
   But for your words, they rob the Hybla bees
   And leave them honeyless.

Antony.   Not stingless too.

Brutus. O, yes, and soundless too.
   For you have stol'n their buzzing, Antony,
   And very wisely threat before you sting.

Antony. Villains, you did not so, when your vile daggers

Hack'd one another in the sides of Cæsar.
You show'd your teeth like apes, and fawn'd like hounds,
And bow'd like bondmen, kissing Cæsar's feet;
Whilst damned Casca, like a cur, behind
Struck Cæsar on the neck. O you flatterers!

Cassius. Flatterers! Now, Brutus, thank yourself:
This tongue had not offended so today,
If Cassius might have ruled.

Octavius. Come, come, the cause. If arguing make us sweat,
The proof of it will turn to redder drops.
Look, I draw a sword against conspirators.
When think you that the sword goes up again?
Never till Cæsar's three and thirty wounds
Be well avenged, or till another Cæsar
Have added slaughter to the sword of traitors.

Brutus. Cæsar, thou canst not die by traitors' hands,
Unless thou bring'st them with thee.

Octavius. So I hope.
I was not born to die on Brutus' sword.

Brutus. O, if thou wert the noblest of thy strain,
Young man, thou couldst not die more honourable.

Cassius. A peevish schoolboy, worthless of such honour,
Join'd with a masker and a reveller!

Antony. Old Cassius still!

Octavius. Come, Antony, away!
Defiance, traitors, hurl we in your teeth.
If you dare fight today, come to the field:
If not, when you have stomachs.

Exeunt Octavius, Antony, *and their army.*

Cassius. Why now, blow wind, swell billow, and swim bark!
The storm is up, and all is on the hazard.

Brutus. Ho, Lucilius! Hark, a word with you.

Lucilius. [*Standing forth*]   My lord?

                                   Brutus *and* Lucilius *converse apart.*

Cassius. Messala!

Messala. [*Standing forth*] What says my general?

Cassius.   Messala,
   This is my birthday; as this very day
   Was Cassius born. Give me thy hand, Messala:
   Be thou my witness that against my will,
   As Pompey was, am I compell'd to set
   Upon one battle all our liberties.
   You know that I held Epicurus strong,
   And his opinion: now I change my mind
   And partly credit things that do presage.
   Coming from Sardis, on our former ensign
   Two mighty eagles fell and there they perch'd,
   Gorging and feeding from our soldiers' hands,
   Who to Philippi here consorted us:
   This morning are they fled away and gone,
   And in their steads do ravens, crows and kites
   Fly o'er our heads and downward look on us
   As we were sickly prey: their shadows seem
   A canopy most fatal, under which
   Our army lies, ready to give up the ghost.

Messala. Believe not so.

Cassius.   I but believe it partly,
   For I am fresh of spirit and resolved
   To meet all perils very constantly.

Brutus. Even so, Lucilius.

Cassius.   Now, most noble Brutus,
   The gods today stand friendly, that we may,

Lovers in peace, lead on our days to age!
But since the affairs of men rest still incertain,
Let's reason with the worst that may befall.
If we do lose this battle, then is this
The very last time we shall speak together.
What are you then determined to do?

Brutus. Even by the rule of that philosophy
By which I did blame Cato for the death
Which he did give himself—I know not how,
But I do find it cowardly and vile,
For fear of what might fall, so to prevent
The time of life—arming myself with patience
To stay the providence of some high powers
That govern us below.

Cassius.   Then, if we lose this battle,
You are contented to be led in triumph
Through the streets of Rome?

Brutus. No, Cassius, no: think not, thou noble Roman,
That ever Brutus will go bound to Rome.
He bears too great a mind. But this same day
Must end that work the Ideas of March begun,
And whether we shall meet again I know not.
Therefore our everlasting farewell take.
For ever and for ever farewell, Cassius!
If we do meet again, why, we shall smile;
If not, why then this parting was well made.

Cassius. For ever and for ever farewell, Brutus!
If we do meet again, we'll smile indeed;
If not, 'tis true this parting was well made.

Brutus. Why then, lead on. O, that a man might know
The end of this day's business ere it come!

But it sufficeth that the day will end,
And then the end is known. Come, ho! Away!

Exeunt.

scene 2. [*The field of battle*]

Alarum. Enter Brutus *and* Messala

Brutus. Ride, ride, Messala, ride, and give these bills
Unto the legions on the other side.

Loud alarum.

Let them set on at once, for I perceive
But cold demeanour in Octavius' wing,
And sudden push gives them the overthrow.
Ride, ride, Messala: let them all come down.

Exeunt.

scene 3. [*Another part of the field*]

Alarums. Enter Cassius *and* Titinius

Cassius. O look, Titinius, look, the villains fly!
Myself have to mine own turn'd enemy:
This ensign here of mine was turning back;
I slew the coward and did take it from him.

Titinius. O Cassius, Brutus gave the word too early,
Who having some advantage on Octavius,
Took it too eagerly: his soldiers fell to spoil,
Whilst we by Antony are all enclosed.

Enter Pindarus

Pindarus. Fly further off, my lord, fly further off;
 Mark Antony is in your tents, my lord:
 Fly, therefore, noble Cassius, fly far off.

Cassius. This hill is far enough. Look, look, Titinius;
 Are those my tents where I perceive the fire?

Titinius. They are, my lord.

Cassius.   Titinius, if thou lovest me,
 Mount thou my horse and hide thy spurs in him,
 Till he have brought thee up to yonder troops
 And here again, that I may rest assured
 Whether yond troops are friend or enemy.

Titinius. I will be here again, even with a thought.

               Exit.

Cassius. Go, Pindarus, get higher on that hill;
 My sight was ever thick. Regard Titinius,
 And tell me what thou notest about the field.

          Pindarus *ascends the hill.*

 This day I breathed first. Time is come round,
 And where I did begin, there shall I end;
 My life is run his compass. Sirrah, what news?

Pindarus. [*Above*] O my lord!

Cassius. What news?

Pindarus. [*Above*] Titinius is enclosed round about
 With horsemen, that make to him on the spur,
 Yet he spurs on. Now they are almost on him.
 Now, Titinius! Now some light. O, he lights too.
 He's ta'en. [*Shout*] And hark! They shout for joy.

Cassius. Come down, behold no more.
 O, coward that I am, to live so long,
 To see my best friend ta'en before my face!

        Pindarus *descends.*

Come hither, sirrah.
In Parthia did I take thee prisoner,
And then I swore thee, saving of thy life,
That whatsoever I did bid thee do,
Thou shouldst attempt it. Come now, keep thine oath.
Now be a freeman, and with this good sword
That ran through Cæsar's bowels, search this bosom.
Stand not to answer: here, take thou the hilts,
And when my face is cover'd, as 'tis now,
Guide thou the sword.

Pindarus stabs him.

Cæsar, thou art revenged,

Even with the sword that kill'd thee.

Dies.

Pindarus. So, I am free, yet would not so have been,
Durst I have done my will. O Cassius!
Far from this country Pindarus shall run,
Where never Roman shall take note of him.

Exit.

Re-enter Titinius with Messala

Messala. It is but change, Titinius, for Octavius
Is overthrown by noble Brutus' power,
As Cassius' legions are by Antony.

Titinius. These tidings will well comfort Cassius.

Messala. Where did you leave him?

Titinius.   All disconsolate,
With Pindarus his bondman, on this hill.

Messala. Is not that he that lies upon the ground?

Titinius. He lies not like the living. O my heart!

Messala. Is not that he?

Titinius.　　　　　No, this was he, Messala,
　　But Cassius is no more: O setting sun,
　　As in thy red rays thou dost sink tonight,
　　So in his red blood Cassius' day is set,
　　The sun of Rome is set! Our day is gone;
　　Clouds, dews and dangers come. Our deeds are done!
　　Mistrust of my success hath done this deed.

Messala. Mistrust of good success hath done this deed.
　　O hateful Error, Melancholy's child,
　　Why dost thou show to the apt thoughts of men
　　The things that are not? O Error, soon conceived,
　　Thou never comest unto a happy birth,
　　But kill'st the mother that engender'd thee!

Titinius. What, Pindarus! Where art thou, Pindarus?

Messala. Seek him, Titinius, whilst I go to meet
　　The noble Brutus, thrusting this report
　　Into his ears. I may say 'thrusting' it,
　　For piercing steel and darts envenomed
　　Shall be as welcome to the ears of Brutus
　　As tidings of this sight.

Titinius.　　　　　Hie you, Messala,
　　And I will seek for Pindarus the while.

　　　　　　　　　　　　　　　　　Exit Messala.

　　Why didst thou send me forth, brave Cassius?
　　Did I not meet thy friends, and did not they
　　Put on my brows this wreath of victory
　　And bid me give it thee? Didst thou not hear their shouts?
　　Alas, thou hast misconstrued everything!
　　But hold thee, take this garland on thy brow;
　　Thy Brutus bid me give it thee, and I
　　Will do his bidding. Brutus, come apace,
　　And see how I regarded Caius Cassius.

By your leave, gods. This is a Roman's part:
Come, Cassius' sword, and find Titinius' heart.

Kills himself.

Alarum. Re-enter Messala, *with* Brutus,
young Cato, *and others*

Brutus. Where, where, Messala, doth his body lie?

Messala. Lo, yonder, and Titinius mourning it.

Brutus. Titinius' face is upward.

Cato.   He is slain.

Brutus. O Julius Cæsar, thou art mighty yet!
    Thy spirit walks abroad and turns our swords
    In our own proper entrails.

Low alarums.

Cato.   Brave Titinius!
    Look whether he have not crown'd dead Cassius!

Brutus. Are yet two Romans living such as these?
    The last of all the Romans, fare thee well!
    It is impossible that ever Rome
    Should breed thy fellow. Friends, I owe mo'e tears
    To this dead man than you shall see me pay.
    I shall find time, Cassius, I shall find time.
    Come therefore, and to Thasos send his body.
    His funerals shall not be in our camp,
    Lest it discomfort us. Lucilius, come,
    And come, young Cato: let us to the field.
    Labeo and Flavius set our battles on.
    'Tis three o'clock; and, Romans, yet ere night
    We shall try fortune in a second fight.

Exeunt.

scene 4.   [*Another part of the field*]

Alarum. Enter, fighting, Soldiers *of both armies;
then* Brutus, *young* Cato, Lucilius, *and others*

Brutus. Yet, countrymen, O yet hold up your heads!

Cato. What bastard doth not? Who will go with me?
   I will proclaim my name about the field.
   I am the son of Marcus Cato, ho!
   A foe to tyrants, and my country's friend.
   I am the son of Marcus Cato, ho!

Brutus. And I am Brutus, Marcus Brutus, I,
   Brutus, my country's friend; know me for Brutus!

                                                                    Cato *is killed.*

Lucilius. O young and noble Cato, art thou down?
   Why, now thou diest as bravely as Titinius,
   And mayst be honour'd, being Cato's son.

First Soldier. Yield, or thou diest.

Lucilius.   Only I yield to die:
   There is so much that thou wilt kill me straight;
   Kill Brutus, and be honour'd in his death.

First Soldier. We must not. A noble prisoner!

Second Soldier. Room, ho! Tell Antony, Brutus is ta'en.

First Soldier. I'll tell the news. Here comes the general.

                         Enter Antony

   Brutus is ta'en, Brutus is ta'en, my lord.

Antony. Where is he?

Lucilius. Safe, Antony; Brutus is safe enough.
   I dare assure thee that no enemy

Shall ever take alive the noble Brutus:
The gods defend him from so great a shame!
When you do find him, or alive or dead,
He will be found like Brutus, like himself.

Antony. This is not Brutus, friend, but, I assure you,
A prize no less in worth. Keep this man safe,
Give him all kindness. I had rather have
Such men my friends than enemies. Go on,
And see whether Brutus be alive or dead,
And bring us word unto Octavius' tent
How everything is chanced.

Exeunt.

scene 5. [*Another part of the field*]

Enter Brutus, Dardanius, Clitus, Strato, *and* Volumnius

Brutus. Come, poor remains of friends, rest on this rock.

Clitus. Statilius show'd the torch-light, but, my lord,
He came not back. He is or ta'en or slain.

Brutus. Sit thee down, Clitus. Slaying is the word.
It is a deed in fashion. Hark thee, Clitus.

Whispering.

Clitus. What, I, my lord? No, not for all the world.

Brutus. Peace then, no words.

Clitus.   I'll rather kill myself.

Brutus. Hark thee, Dardanius.

Whispering.

Dardanius.   Shall I do such a deed?

Clitus. O Dardanius!

Dardanius. O Clitus!

Clitus. What ill request did Brutus make to thee?

Dardanius. To kill him, Clitus. Look, he meditates.

Clitus. Now is that noble vessel full of grief,
 That it runs over even at his eyes.

Brutus. Come hither, good Volumnius, list a word.

Volumnius. What says my lord?

Brutus.   Why this, Volumnius:
 The ghost of Cæsar hath appear'd to me
 Two several times by night—at Sardis once,
 And this last night here in Philippi fields:
 I know my hour is come.

Volumnius.   Not so, my lord.

Brutus. Nay, I am sure it is, Volumnius.
 Thou seest the world, Volumnius, how it goes.
 Our enemies have beat us to the pit.

              Low alarums.

 It is more worthy to leap in ourselves
 Than tarry till they push us. Good Volumnius,
 Thou know'st that we two went to school together:
 Even for that our love of old, I prithee
 Hold thou my sword-hilts whilst I run on it.

Volumnius. That's not an office for a friend, my lord.

              Alarum still.

Clitus. Fly, fly, my lord, there is no tarrying here.

Brutus. Farewell to you; and you; and you, Volumnius.
 Strato, thou hast been all this while asleep;
 Farewell to thee too, Strato. Countrymen,
 My heart doth joy that yet in all my life
 I found no man but he was true to me.

I shall have glory by this losing day,
More than Octavius and Mark Antony
By this vile conquest shall attain unto.
So fare you well at once, for Brutus' tongue
Hath almost ended his life's history:
Night hangs upon mine eyes; my bones would rest,
That have but labour'd to attain this hour.

Alarum. Cry within, 'Fly, fly, fly!'

Clitus. Fly, my lord, fly!

Brutus.   Hence! I will follow.

Exeunt Clitus, Dardanius, *and* Volumnius.

I prithee, Strato, stay thou by thy lord.
Thou art a fellow of a good respect;
Thy life hath had some smatch of honour in it.
Hold then my sword, and turn away thy face,
While I do run upon it. Wilt thou, Strato?

Strato. Give me your hand first. Fare you well, my lord.

Brutus. Farewell, good Strato. [*Runs on his sword.*] Cæsar, now be
still:
I kill'd not thee with half so good a will.

Dies.

Alarum. Retreat. Enter Octavius, Antony, Messala,
Lucilius, *and the army*

Octavius. What man is that?

Messala. My master's man. Strato, where is thy master?

Strato. Free from the bondage you are in, Messala.
The conquerors can but make a fire of him,
For Brutus only overcame himself
And no man else hath honour by his death.

Lucilius. So Brutus should be found. I thank thee, Brutus,
That thou hast proved Lucilius' saying true.

Octavius. All that served Brutus, I will entertain them.
Fellow, wilt thou bestow thy time with me?

Strato. Ay, if Messala will prefer me to you.

Octavius. Do so, good Messala.

Messala. How died my master, Strato?

Strato. I held the sword, and he did run on it.

Messala. Octavius, then take him to follow thee,
That did the latest service to my master.

Antony. This was the noblest Roman of them all:
All the conspirators, save only he
Did that they did in envy of great Cæsar.
He only, in a general honest thought
And common good to all, made one of them.
His life was gentle, and the elements
So mix'd in him that Nature might stand up
And say to all the world 'This was a man!'

Octavius. According to his virtue let us use him,
With all respect and rites of burial.
Within my tent his bones tonight shall lie,
Most like a soldier, order'd honourably.
So call the field to rest, and let's away,
To part the glories of this happy day.

Exeunt.